SHEPHERD'S NOTES

SHEPHERD'S NOTES

Bible Summary Series

Life & Letters of Paul

BROADMAN
&HOLMAN
PUBLISHERS

Nashville, Tennessee

0–8054—9385–9
Dewey Decimal Classification: 225.9
Subject Heading: Paul, the Apostle, Saint.
Library of Congress Card Catalog Number: 99–054866

Library of Congress Cataloging-in-Publication Data

Gould, Dana, 1951–
      The life and letters of Paul/ by Dana Gould.
          p.   cm.   — (Shepherd's notes.)
      Includes bibliographical references.
      ISBN 0–8054–9385–9
      1. Paul, the Apostle, Saint.   2. Bible. N.T. Epistles of Paul—Criticism, interpretation, etc.   3. Bible. N.T. Acts—Criticism, interpretation. etc.   I. Title. II. Series.
      BS2505.A3 G68   2000
      225.9'2—dc21   99–054866
                                                                              CIP

                    1 2 3 4 5 6   03 02 01 00
                                R

CONTENTS

DESIGNED FOR THE BUSY USER

Shepherd's Notes is designed to provide an easy-to-use tool for getting a quick handle on a Bible book's important features, and in the case of this volume of gaining an understanding of the life and letters of Paul. Information available in more difficult-to-use reference works has been incorporated into the *Shepherd's Notes* format. This brings you the benefits of many more advanced and expensive works packed into one small volume.

Shepherd's Notes are for laymen, pastors, teachers, small group leaders and participants, as well as the classroom student. Enrich your personal study or quiet time. Shorten your class or small group preparation time as you gain valuable insights in the truths of God's Word that you can pass along to your students or group members.

DESIGNED FOR QUICK ACCESS

Those with time restraints will especially appreciate the timesaving features built in the *Shepherd's Notes*.

Concise Information. The writings of Paul and the Acts of the Apostles are replete with characters, places, events, and teachings that will enrich believers. Short sections provide quick "snapshots" of Paul's life and thought.

Icons. Various icons in the margin highlight recurring themes in Paul's writings and aid in selective searching or tracing of those themes.

Sidebars and Charts. These specially selected features provide additional background information to your study or preparation. These include definitions as well as cultural, historical, and biblical insights.

In addition to the above features, for those readers who require or desire more information and resources for studying Paul's writings, a list of reference sources used for this volume suggests many works that allow the reader to extend the scope of his or her study of the Acts and Paul's letters.

DESIGNED TO WORK FOR YOU

Personal Study. Using the *Shepherd's Notes* with a passage of Scripture can enlighten your study and take it to a new level. At your fingertips is information that would require searching several volumes to find. In addition, many points of application occur throughout the volume, contributing to personal growth.

Teaching. A running outline frames the text of Paul's writings and provide a logical presentation of the message. Historical Context and other icons indicate where background information is supplied.

Group Study. Shepherd's Notes can be an excellent companion volume to use for gaining a quick but accurate understanding of Paul and his writings. The *Note's* format provides a summary of Paul's life and influence that is helpful in doing more detailed study in either Acts or in particular letters of Paul.

LIST OF MARGIN ICONS USED IN
THE LIFE AND LETTERS OF PAUL:

 Shepherd's Notes. Placed to indicate a New Testament book summary. This is a capsule statement that provides the reader with the essence of the message of that particular book.

 Historical Context. To indicate background information—historical, biographical, cultural—and provide insight on the understanding or interpretation of a passage.

 Old Testament Passage. To indicate a prophecy fulfillment and its discussion in the text.

New Testament Passage. To indicate a New Testament passage that illuminates Paul's life and thought.

 Quote. Used to identify an enlightening quote pertinent to the discussion of the text.

 Word Picture. Indicates that the meaning of a specific word or phrase is illustrated so as to shed light on it.

SECTION ONE: INTRODUCTION

THE LIFE AND WRITINGS OF PAUL

The Importance of Paul and His Writings

Paul was an outstanding missionary and writer of the early church. Paul the apostle and his theology are important to the New Testament not only because thirteen epistles bear his name, but also because of the extended biographical information given in the book of Acts. From the information in these two sources, we piece together a reasonable picture of one of the major personalities of early Christianity.

Why Study the Life and Writings of Paul?
Paul's Place in Christianity

A strong case has been made for the fact that the most significant event in the New Testament following the descent of the Holy Spirit at Pentecost is the conversion of Saul of Tarsus. In Acts, Luke gives three separate accounts of Paul's conversion.

Try to imagine the Acts of the Apostles without Paul. Or try to think of the New Testament without the letters of Paul.

Paul played a role in the history of Christianity that was unique. It is difficult to conceive of the development of Christianity apart from this gifted and complex man.

It is often said that we see God's providence best in retrospect. That is certainly the case in the life of Paul. Looking back, we can see clearly the hand of God in the circumstances of Paul's birth and early life in the same way God guided the development of other leaders He called.

"Before I formed you in the womb I knew you, before you were born I set you apart; I appointed you as a prophet to the nations" (Jer. 1:5).

PAUL'S EARLY LIFE AND TRAINING (A.D. 1–35)(ACTS 7:58–12:25)

His Early Life

Paul's Jewish name was Saul, given at birth after his father or some near kin, or even after the famous Old Testament King Saul, who like Paul was from the tribe of Benjamin. Having been born in a Roman city and claiming Roman citizenship, Paul (*Paulos*) was his official Roman name. Normally, a citizen would have three names similar to our first, middle, and last name. Paul would have been the middle or last name, since the first name was usually indicated only by the initial.

Tarsus, the place of Paul's birth (Acts 22:3), was a bustling city a few miles inland from the Mediterranean on Turkey's southern shore. By Paul's day it was a self-governing city, loyal to the Roman Empire. We do not know how Paul's parents or forebears came to live in Tarsus. Many Jewish families emigrated from their homeland willingly or as a result of foreign intervention in the centuries before Christ. Tradition says that Paul's parents migrated from a village in Galilee, but this cannot be verified.

HIS YOUTH AND EDUCATION (ACTS 21:39; 22:3; 23:6, 34; 26:4–5; ROM. 11:1; 2 COR. 11:22; GAL. 1:13–14; PHIL. 3:4–5).

Growing up in a Jewish family meant that Paul was well trained in the Jewish Scriptures and tradition (Acts 26:4–8; Phil. 3:5–6) beginning in the home with the celebration of the Jewish holidays: Passover, Yom Kippur, Hanukkah, and others. At an early age he entered the synagogue day school. Here he learned to read and write by copying select passages of Scripture. He learned the ancient Hebrew language from the Hebrew

Scriptures. At home his parents probably spoke the current dialect—Aramaic. As Paul related to the larger community, he learned the Greek language. Every Jewish boy also learned a trade. Paul learned the art of tentmaking which he later used as a means of sustenance (Acts 18:3).

Paul eventually went to Jerusalem to study under the famous rabbi, Gamaliel. He was probably thirteen to eighteen years old.

His Character (Phil. 3:6; 1 Tim. 1:12–13; 2 Tim. 1:3)

Saul was an intense person both before and after his conversion. He was zealous for God (Acts 22:3) and for God's will as revealed in the Mosaic Law. He was no rebellious son indulging in the sins of the Gentiles. Saul was straight as an arrow and had been known as a person of exemplary behavior since he was a boy. The idolatries and corruption of the Greco-Roman world were deeply offensive to his conscience. Paul, like his teacher Gamaliel and like his father (Acts 23:6), became a Pharisee.

SAUL, THE PERSECUTOR

If the behavior of many of the Gentiles was offensive to Saul, even more disturbing was a sect which came to be called the Way. Followers of the Way, most of whom were Jewish, claimed Israel's Messiah had come in Jesus of Nazareth. Saul believed Jesus and His teachings didn't match up with what Messiah would be. In his zeal for God and God's law, he became a feared persecutor of the Way. There are no less than eight passages that make allusion to this sad period in Paul's life.

Gamaliel was the grandson of the great Rabbi Hillel. Although he was a Pharisee, he was not the zealot that his pupil Paul was early in his adult life. Gamaliel squelched a plan by the Sanhedrin to kill the apostles by reminding the members that interference with what the apostles were doing might prove to be opposition to God (Acts 5:34).

Paul made havoc of the church—"began to destroy the church" (Acts 8:3). Literally, the word *destroy* means that "he was ravaging" the church. No stronger metaphor could well have been used.

Luke paints a picture of great contrasts that likely made a deep impression on the young Rabbi Saul. On the one hand there is a mob seething with anger and out of control in their stoning of a man who calmly looks to heaven and sees the risen Christ at the right hand of God. Stephen was a man at peace with God and even with his enemies.

Stephen

Stephen was the first Christian martyr. His name means "crown." Stephen was in the forefront of those who saw Christianity as much more than a Jewish sect.

STEPHEN'S DEATH
(ACTS 7:57–58; 8:1–2; 22:20)

Luke introduces Saul in Acts at the execution of Stephen, a follower of and eloquent spokeman for the Way. Stephen preached Jesus as Messiah. He debated with Jewish leaders from several provinces including Cilicia, Saul's province. It may have been in this context that Saul first encountered Stephen.

Saul and Stephen would have disagreed on (1) who Jesus was, and (2) what the place of the law was in making a person right with God.

GENERAL PERSECUTIONS
(ACTS 8:3–4; 22:4–5, 19; 26:9–11)

The Severity of the Persecution. Luke dates a severe persecution of Christians from the day of Stephen's execution. Participating in Stephen's death caused Saul to become even more intense and violent in opposition to Christians. For Saul, stopping this movement became an obsession. Luke describes him as "breathing out murderous threats against the Lord's disciples" (Acts 9:1).

Following his miraculous conversion to Christ, Paul suffered greatly over the next years of his life as he remembered these activities.

PAUL'S CONVERSION (A.D. 36)

On one occasion not long after Stephen's death, Saul got letters from the high priest which empowered him to go to Damascus and arrest any people he found who were followers of Jesus. He would then bring them to Jerusalem to be punished.

On the Road to Damascus (Acts 9:1–9; 22:5–11; 26:12–20). As Saul and his companions approached Damascus, he was suddenly surrounded by a light brighter than the sun—so bright that he and his companions fell to the ground. There on the ground Saul heard a voice speaking to him in Hebrew: "Saul, Saul, why do you persecute me?"

Saul asked the One speaking to identify Himself. The voice told Saul He was Jesus—the very One Saul had been persecuting. Saul then asked Jesus what He wanted Saul to do. Jesus commanded Saul to go on to Damascus. He would be told there what to do next.

The experience of this great light impaired Saul's vision to such an extent that his companions had to lead him the rest of the way to Damascus. For three days, Saul stayed in the house of a man named Judas on Strait Street in Damascus. He was without sight and did not eat or drink during this time.

Paul and Ananias (Acts 9:10–19; 22:12–16). At some point during the three days Saul was waiting at the home of Judas, the Lord spoke to a disciple named Ananias, whom Paul later describes as "a godly man in his devotion to the law" (Acts 22:12, NLT). The Lord told Ananias to go to Judas' house and ask for Saul. Ananias was told that Saul would be expecting him because the Lord was appearing to Saul in a vision to tell him Ananias would call on him.

Ananias hesitated. He told the Lord that he had heard about Saul and the evil he had done to Jesus' followers. The Lord responded with a command: "Go!" Ananias obeyed. He found Saul and laid his hands on him. Saul's blindness disappeared and he received the Holy Spirit. He was then baptized and took food for the first time since his experience on the Damascus road.

Accounts of Paul's Conversion in His Letters. Both his conversion and call are reflected in Paul's

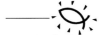

Paul's Confession in the Epistles.

In Paul's letters, we find confessions of his involvement in persecuting the church. "For I am the least of the apostles, who am not fit to be called an apostle, because I persecuted the church of God" (1 Cor. 15:9, NASB); "I was formerly a blasphemer and a persecutor and a violent aggressor" (1 Tim. 1:13, NASB). Other refererences are in Galatians 1:13, 22–24; Philippians 3:6.

"But the Lord said, 'Go and do what I say. For Saul is my chosen instrument to take my message to the Gentiles and to kings, as well as to the people of Israel. And I will show him how much he must suffer for me'" (Acts 9:15–16, NLT).

letters. He wrote that Jesus had appeared to him (1 Cor.15:8–10; 9:1); the gospel Paul preached had come by revelation (Gal.1:12); he had been called by God (Gal.1:1; Eph.3:2–12). His conversion brought a complete change in the inner controlling power of his life. It was like dying and receiving a new life (Gal.2:20) or being created anew (2 Cor. 5:17–20). Romans 7–8 speaks of Paul's spiritual condition before his conversion. This experience of radical change and call to the Gentiles provided the motivation to travel throughout the Roman world as the Apostle to the Gentiles.

In Galatians 1:15–16, three separate stages appear in the history of the apostle's consecration to his ministry:

1. First, the predestination to his high office, which dated from before his birth ("who set me apart from birth").
2. The conversion and call to the apostleship, which took place on the way to Damascus, Acts 9:3 ("called me by his grace").
3. The entering upon his ministry in fulfillment of this call (Acts 9:20; 13:2–3) ("To reveal his Son in me so that I might preach him among the Gentiles").

PAUL IN DAMASCUS AND ARABIA (A.D. 37–39) (ACTS 9:17–26; 26:15–20; 2 COR. 11:32–33)

After his baptism by Ananias, Paul "spent several days with the disciples in Damascus" (Acts 9:19). He was soon afforded the opportunity to preach in the synagogues, which he did, achieving great success as a disputant and increasing in strength (Acts 9:20–22). Then followed the journey into Arabia (Gal. 1:17), from where he returned to Damascus, from which city, after meeting with great opposition from the Jews, who tried to kill him, he escaped to Jerusalem.

Neither Luke nor Paul gives any details of the time spent in Arabia. Given the radical change that had taken place in Saul's life, one can well imagine that this was a time of reading, prayer, and meditation with a view to assimilating his experience with the risen Christ and seeing what changes this experience entailed for his understanding of God and himself.

PAUL'S FIRST VISIT TO JERUSALEM (A.D. 39) (ACTS 9:26–29; 22:15–21; GAL. 1:17–20)

(Duration: 15 days)

Paul's first visit to Jerusalem, which was of great importance in his life, is given quite fully here. In Galatians the time is specified as fifteen days, and the apostles whom he met are limited to Peter and James (Acts 9:27). None would give the impression that Paul saw *all* the apostles, but the limiting expression in Galatians (1:9) seems to imply that the rest were away on preaching tours or were otherwise prevented from meeting him.

As might be expected, Paul was not given a warm welcome by the disciples in Jerusalem. Many doubted his sincerity and feared that his purpose was to spy on Christians. At this point, Barnabas became his advocate, gaining acceptance for him among the Christians in Jerusalem.

Warned in a Vision in the Temple. In his speech on the stairs of Antonio Fortress nearly 20 years later, Paul spoke of a vision in the Temple (Acts 22:17–21) that occurred during his first visit to Jerusalem. In Acts 22:16, Paul narrates the account of his baptism by Ananias, and then adds

"There is some doubt as to the precise place of his retirement, because Arabia is a word of vague and variable significance. But most probably it denotes the Arabia of the Wanderings, the principal feature of which was Mount Sinai. . . . Here Moses had seen the burning bush and communed with God on the top of the Mountain. Here Elijah had roamed in his season of despair and drunk anew at the wells of inspiration" —James A. Stalker from *The Life of St. Paul*, (Fleming H. Revell, 1950), 46.

"But Barnabas took him and brought him to the apostles. He told them how Saul on his journey had seen the Lord and that the Lord had spoken to him, and how in Damascus he had preached fearlessly in the name of Jesus" (Acts 9:27).

in verse 17, "When I returned to Jerusalem and was praying at the temple, I fell into a trance and saw the Lord speaking. 'Quick! . . . Leave Jerusalem immediately, because they will not accept your testimony about me.'"

According to Luke, Paul left the city because of the concern of his friends (Acts 9:30). Paul, however, gives the more personal and spiritual reason, that of a supernatural vision in the Temple (Acts 22:17–21). It is a mark of truth that we find Luke stating the outward impulse: the apostle the inward ground.

PAUL IN CAESAREA AND TARSUS (39–43 A.D.)

(Duration: 4 or 5 years)

Preaching in Syria and Cilicia. Paul was taken from Jerusalem to Caesarea. From Caesarea, he returned to his native province of Cilicia. Luke's account makes it sound like Paul went immediately and directly to Cilicia, but it could well be that he went by way of Syria where he preached (Gal. 1:21–24).

PAUL IN TARSUS AND ANTIOCH

The persecution of the church that intensified with the death of Stephen led to a dispersion of Christians—first throughout Judea and Samaria. Next, these disciples went as far as Phoenecia, Cyprus, and Antioch in Syria. As they went, these followers of Jesus preached the gospel to fellow Jews. Eventually, some disciples from Cyprus and North Africa came to Antioch in Syria. There they proclaimed Jesus as Messiah to Gentiles as well as Jews. The result was that Gentiles became believers.

The church at Jerusalem heard about this. They sent Barnabas to Antioch to take a first-hand look at what was happening. Barnabas was gratified at

Caesarea

Located on the Mediterranean Sea twenty-three miles south of Mount Carmel is the city of Caesarea.The city appears in the book of Acts as a place of witness, travel, and the seat of government. Philip, having witnessed to the Ethiopian eunuch, is mentioned as arriving at Caesarea after a preaching mission. Peter led a centurion, Cornelius, who was stationed there, to become a Christian. Paul had several reported contacts with the city as a port, and perhaps as a place of imprisonment and trial. Herod Agrippa I had a residence there and died there.

evidences of God's hand at work among the Gentiles in Antioch. He encouraged them to continue what they were doing and to be wholehearted in their obedience to the Lord. The result was that a great number of people came to the Lord.

Barnabas, a Spirit-filled man, recognized a need as he observed the reception of the gospel by the Gentiles in Antioch. Heretofore, only Jews had become believers. They read the same Scriptures as Jesus read. Now people with no knowledge of the God of Abraham, Isaac, Jacob, Moses, David, and the prophets were coming to faith in Jesus as Messiah and Lord. What would happen to them unless they understood the context in which Jesus had been sent?

Barnabas was a Levite from Cyprus whose given name was Joseph. He sold property and gave the proceeds to the church in Jerusalem. The disciples gave him the name Barnabas, meaning "son of encouragement" or "son of exhortation."

Barnabas knew just the man for this task: Saul of Tarsus. In his first meeting with him in Jerusalem, he was no doubt impressed that a Jewish leader of his learning and zeal for the Law had come to faith in Jesus. Also, he himself may have been greatly enriched as Paul articulated to him the gospel of Jesus and its foundation in the Hebrew Scriptures. Not only was Paul a Hebrew of the Hebrews, he had been raised in Tarsus, a cosmopolitan Gentile city. Paul was sensitive to cultural differences and could communicate appropriately to a variety of cultures.

So Barnabas set out for Tarsus where he found Paul (Acts 11:25). Saul recognized the voice of God in the words of Barnabas, and the two friends traveled in all haste to Antioch.

The "whole year" spent in Antioch was that of A.D. 44, since it was the year which preceded Paul's second journey to Jerusalem, at the time of the famine.

PAUL'S FIRST MISSIONARY JOURNEY AND RESIDENCE IN ANTIOCH (A.D. 47–49) (ACTS 13:1–14:28)

(Duration: About two years)

THE CALL

Barnabas and Saul were two among five prophets and teachers Luke mentions as serving together in the church at Antioch. As they worshiped and prayed, the Holy Spirit spoke through one or more of the prophets with instructions that Barnabas and Saul should be set apart for a special assignment. The church prayed, fasted, laid their hands on Saul and Barnabas, and sent them on their way.

Salamis is on the eastern coast of Cyprus. The journey from Seleucia to Salamis is seventy miles.

The Holy Spirit guided Barnabas and Saul to Selucia Pieria, the port city of Antioch, about 25 miles southwest of Antioch on the Mediterranean coast. From there they sailed to Cyprus, home of Barnabas and a large Jewish community.

IN CYPRUS (ACTS 13:4–13)

The journey from Salamis to Paphos was approximately 115 miles. A Roman road across the southern part of the island was then the most direct route.

Preaching at Salamis (Acts 13:4–5). The Jews who had immigrated to Cyprus had established their synagogues, where they maintained regular worship. Luke gives few details and only states that Paul and Barnabas proclaimed the gospel in the synagogue in Salamis. This is the first time Luke mentions John Mark's traveling with them. It isn't clear whether he was with them in Antioch or joined them in Salamis. Since John Mark was Barnabas' cousin and Barnabas was from Cyprus, John Mark may have joined them in Salamis.

The Sorcerer at Paphos (Acts 13:6–12). Apparently Barnabas and Saul did not stay long in Salamis. They journeyed by land to Paphos, a port on the westernmost tip of Cyprus.

Paphos was the Roman capital of Cyprus. It was there that the proconsul, Sergius Paulus, lived. He is described as a "man of understanding," though under the influence of Elymas the sorcerer. In their effort to win Sergius Paulus to Christ, the apostle encountered the determined opposition of Elymas. Finally, Paul challenged this "son of the devil" and caused him to be blinded for a season. Sergius Paulus was impressed and believed.

Paul's Name Change (Acts 13:9). Why was Saul's name changed to Paul? It is probable that Paul acquired this name like other Jews in that age, who, when they associated with foreigners, had often two names—the one Jewish, the other foreign (Gentile). This explanation of the origin of the name accounts for its introduction at this stage of the history. It is here for the first time that Luke speaks directly of Paul's labors among the heathen; and it is natural that he should apply to him the name by which he was chiefly known in that sphere of his ministry.

The voyage from Paphos to Perga (southern Turkey today) was 175 miles. The port city where they probably landed was Attalia—a distance of twelve miles from Perga, the capital city of the Roman province that was made up of Pamphilia and Lycia.

Perga in Pamphilia (Acts 13:13). The missionaries now left Paphos for Perga. It was at this time that John Mark forsook them, and taking advantage of some vessel which was sailing towards Palestine, returned to Jerusalem, which had been his home in earlier years (Acts 12:12, 25). Luke is silent on why Mark left the mission at this point.

S. Mitchell suggests a reason why Paul and Barnabas were drawn to Pisidian Antioch: "Inscriptions have been discovered at Antioch to various members of the Paullus family. One mentions a Sergia Paulla and dates shortly after Paul's visit there. It is possible that she was a daughter of the Cypriot governor and that he suggested that Paul witness in this area where he had family"—Quoted in "Paul and His Letters" by John Polhill, *Anchor Bible Dictionary*, 88.

Paul expressed a principle that he followed in city after city. He told the crowd: "It was necessary that the word of God should be spoken to you first; since you repudiate it, and judge yourselves unworthy of eternal life, behold, we are turning to the Gentiles" (Acts 13: 46, NASB).

IN ANTIOCH IN PISIDIA (ACTS 13:14–50; GAL. 4:13–15)

Paul and Barnabas next traveled the 100 miles north of Perga to Pisidian Antioch.

Paul's Address (Acts 13:14–41). On the Sabbath they went to the Synagogue. After the Scriptures were read, Paul and Barnabas were invited to give a word of exhortation to the assembly. Paul accepted the invitation and addressed the synagogue. He sketched a history of God's dealing with Israel. He then presented Jesus as Israel's Messiah, the promised offspring of David.

Paul and Barnabas Rejected (Acts 13:42–49). The worshipers wanted to hear more and urged Paul and Barnabas to come back next Sabbath. When the leaders of the Synagogue saw the large crowd that returned on the next Sabbath, they became jealous and began arguing against Paul's message. The apostles, promptly recognizing the willingness of the Gentiles and the unbelief of the Jews, turned at once and without reserve to the Gentiles. It is the course that Paul himself defines in his epistle to the Romans, when he describes the gospel as coming first to the Jew and then to the Gentile (Rom. 1:16).

The Departure from Antioch Because of Persecution (Acts 13:50). Angrily the Jews turned against Paul and Barnabas. The persecution became so severe that the two men were chased out of the city. In spite of the opposition, Luke tells us that the new believers in Pisidian Antioch were filled with the Holy Spirit and were joyful.

PAUL IN ICONIUM
(ACTS 13:51–52; 14:1–6)

Paul and Barnabas traveled eastward on a road known as the "imperial road." This road led from Pisidian Antioch to Lystra, another Roman colony. Rather than going directly to Lystra, Paul and Barnabas made an intermediate stop at Iconium.

Paul and Barnabas Persecuted (Acts 13:51–52; 14:1–5). At Iconium the two missionaries were well received initially. Many Jews and Gentiles became believers as a result of their powerful preaching. God also empowered them to do signs and wonders among the people of Iconium. Some of the Jews who didn't believe sowed seeds of distrust among the Gentiles. The result was a divided city regarding the message of Paul and Barnabas. Those who opposed them planned to stone them. When Paul and Barnabas learned about this plot, they left Iconium for the region of Lycaonia, in which the major cities were Lystra and Derbe.

IN LYSTRA
(ACTS 14:6–20; 2 COR. 11:24–25)

Paul Heals a Lame Man (Acts 14:6–13). The event that caught the attention of the indifferent Gentiles of the city was Paul's healing of a poor, crippled man. As Paul preached, his eye fell on a crippled man in the audience. Paul saw that the man had faith to be healed and so commanded him to stand up. The man, crippled from birth, jumped up and began to walk. The reaction was instant. Such a cure of a congenital disease, so sudden and so complete, would have confounded the most skillful and skeptical physician. An illiterate people would be filled with astonishment, and rush immediately to the conclusion that supernatural powers were present

Iconium

Iconium's location is that of the modern Turkish provincial capital Konya. Iconium was mentioned for the first time in the fourth century B.C. by the historian Xenophon. In New Testament times it was considered part of the Roman province of Galatia. Evidently it has had a continuous existence since its founding.

Lystra

Lystra was the home of Timothy, a young man who would become Paul's son in the ministry. Paul and Barnabas may well have stayed in the home of Timothy, his mother, Eunice, and grandmother, Lois.

13

among them. These Lycaonians thought at once of their native traditions, and crying out in their mother tongue—they exclaimed that the gods had again visited them in the likeness of men—that Jupiter and Mercury were again in Lycaonia—that the persuasive speaker was Mercury and his companion Jupiter. They identified Paul with Mercury because of his eloquence.

Paul's Speech (Acts 14:14–18). Paul and Barnabas were horrified at the peoples' reaction to them. They tore their clothes and quickly sought to let the people know that they were humans like them. Paul and Barnabas's message at Lystra demonstrates their skill in cross cultural communications. Here they were addressing people who believed in many gods. They had no understanding of the God of Israel. So the focus was on God as Creator and Sustainer of life. Paul pointed to the tangible gifts God continually gave them and which made them happy. And he said in effect—I'm here to tell you the Good News about the One who provides you with these good gifts.

Even with this explanation, the people kept on wanting to offer sacrifices to Paul and Barnabas.

Paul Is Stoned (Acts 14:19–20). Jews from Pisidian Antioch (100 miles away!) and Iconium didn't forget Paul and Barnabas. They banded together and followed the missionaries to Lystra, stirred up the crowd and stoned Paul. He was stoned in the streets of Lystra, dragged through the city gate, cast outside the walls, and left for dead. Faithful disciples went out to where he was and surrounded him, and he revived and came back to Lystra. From there, Paul and Barnabas traveled eastward to Derbe.

"Men, why are you doing these things? We are also men of the same nature as you, and preach the gospel to you in order that you should turn from these vain things to a living God, who made the heaven and the earth and the sea, and all that is in them. And in the generations gone by He permitted all the nations to go their own ways; and yet He did not leave Himself without witness, in that He did good and gave you rains from heaven and fruitful seasons, satisfying your hears with food and gladness" (Acts 14:15, NASB).

TO DERBE, LYSTRA, ICONIUM, ANTIOCH IN PISIDIA, AND THROUGHOUT PISIDIA, TO PERGA (ACTS 14:20–25)

At this point, the missionaries concluded their first campaign and begin the journey home. For good reasons they decided to end their mission work by retracing their route back to Lystra, Iconium, Pisidian Antioch, and Perga. They wanted to see again their converts in these cities, to give them further instructions, to counsel with them in their work, to organize them into churches, and secure responsible leaders for these churches.

The missionaries took a ship at Attalia and sailed back to Antioch.

PAUL AND BARNABAS TAKE RESIDENCE IN ANTIOCH (ACTS 14:25–28)

Paul and Barnabas stayed a long time with the disciples in Antioch. They reported all that happened in Asia Minor, with special emphasis on the way God "had opened the door of faith to the Gentiles (14:27).

Derbe

Derbe was an important city in the region of Lycaonia in the province of Galatia in Asia Minor. It was apparently near what is modern Kerti Huyuk. The residents of Derbe and Lystra spoke a different language than the people to the north in Iconium. Persecution in Lystra led to a successful preaching mission in Derbe. On the second missionary journey, Paul returned to Derbe. He apparently visited again on the third journey. Paul's fellow minister Gaius was from Derbe.

THE COUNCIL AT JERUSALEM (ACTS 15:1–35)

PAUL AND BARNABAS SENT TO JERUSALEM (ACTS 15:1–3; GAL. 2:1–2)

The conference was held A.D. 50 or 51 (fourteen years after Paul's conversion.) It was the first and in some respects the most important council held in the history of Christendom, though differing widely from the councils of later times.

Certain men came from Judea to Antioch and taught that circumcision was necessary for salvation. Their position was that to receive the gospel one had to be a Jew. Gentiles would have to go through the procedures of becoming a Jew, one step of which, for men, was circumcision

Paul and Barnabas, who had completed their first missionary journey to the Gentiles of Asia Minor, strongly disagreed with this teaching. Those from Judea invited Paul and Barnabas to go back to Jerusalem with them and discuss this issue with the apostles.

They took with them Titus, a young Gentile convert who had not been circumcised. In Jerusalem, these missionaries met with the apostles and elders both in private and public meetings in order to let them know what they had done in their evangelism and church planting with the Gentiles across Asia Minor.

Paul and Barnabas had seen Gentiles believe the gospel, receive the Holy Spirit, and become members of a local church. Circumcision had not been required. Becoming Jewish was not a step to receiving Christ.

When some of the brothers in Jerusalem heard this they responded by asserting that circumcision should be required of Gentiles. Not only that, Gentiles had to keep the Law of Moses. Some of the participants in the council strongly wanted Paul's companion, Titus, to be circumcised. Paul resisted.

After some debate, Peter stood to speak. He indirectly referred to the case of Cornelius, a Roman centurion who had received the Holy Spirit and became a believer without being circumcised. Cornelius had believed the gospel Peter preached. And he had been saved through the grace of the Lord Jesus which Peter proclaimed to him. He was not required to become a Jew.

James, Jesus' half brother and the leading elder of the Jerusalem church, spoke. James was in agreement with Peter on this issue. He pointed back to the prophet Amos who said that the Lord is taking a people from among the Gentiles. In light of this, James urged that Jewish Christians not make it difficult for Gentiles to receive Christ.

For the sake of peace between Jews and Gentile Christians, James asked the council to write a letter to the Gentile Christians urging them to abstain from food offered to idols, from sexual immorality, from the meat of strangled animals, and from blood.

The council reached consensus on this matter. They also sided with Paul in not requiring Titus to be circumcised. The council chose two of their own, Judas (Barsabbas) and Silas, and sent them to Antioch with Paul and Barnabas. The four carried with them a letter from the council to Gentile believers in Antioch, Syria, and Cilicia. The letter expresses the position that Peter and James urged the council to take.

Paul and Barnabas's Mission to the Gentiles Ratified (Gal. 2:3–10). The council was asked not only to

"For it seemed good to the Holy Spirit and to us to lay upon you no greater burden than these essentials" (Acts 15:28, NASB). The letter then goes on to list the four practices from which James urged abstention.

17

decide the question of circumcision and to define the relation between the Jewish and Gentile Christians, but also to settle the personal relation between the Jewish and Gentile apostles and to divide their fields of labor.

The pillars of the Jewish church, James, Peter, and John—whatever their views may have been before—were fully convinced, by the logic of events in which they recognized the hand of God, that Paul and Barnabas had been divinely called as apostles to the Gentiles.

PAUL AND BARNABAS BACK AT ANTIOCH (ACTS 15:30–36; GAL. 2:11–14)

The Apostolic Letter Delivered (Acts 15:30–35). Paul and his companions brought the letter from the council to Antioch. The church at Antioch was greatly encouraged by the decision of the council. Judas and Silas stayed at Antioch for a time, making a strong positive contribution to the fellowship there.

The Quarrel Between Paul and Peter (Gal. 2:11–14). The decision of the council regarding the relationship between Hebrew and Gentile Christians was a critical decision in the history of the church. It went against deeply ingrained views—especially on the part of Jewish Christians. Even Peter, who had played a key leadership role in redefining the relationships of Jews and Gentiles in Christ, took a step backwards.

"When I saw that they were not acting in line with the truth of the gospel, I said to Peter in front of them all, 'You are a Jew, yet you live like a Gentile and not like a Jew. How is it, then, that you force Gentiles to follow Jewish customs?'" (Gal. 2:14).

Peter had been sharing meals with Gentiles at Antioch. When some men from the Jerusalem church came to Antioch, he quit eating with Gentile Christians. Paul rebuked Peter for his hypocrisy which had caused Barnabas to withdraw from table fellowship with Gentile Christians.

PAUL'S SECOND MISSIONARY JOURNEY (A.D. 51–54) (ACTS 15:36–18:23)

(Duration: Three years)

PAUL AND BARNABAS SEPARATE (ACTS 15:36–39)

Paul and Barnabas remained in Antioch for several months. After a time, Paul expressed to Barnabas the desire to go back to the churches that had been planted on their first missionary journey. Barnabas wanted to take John Mark with them, but Paul was strongly opposed to Mark's going.

The disagreement between Paul and Barnabas was so sharp, they decided to go their separate ways. Barnabas took Mark and set sail for Cyprus. Paul asked Silas to join him on what has traditionally been called Paul's second missionary journey.

Rather than retracing the route by sea, Paul and Silas traveled over land. Luke says that as they traveled through Syria and Paul's home province of Cilicia, they strengthened the churches. The New Testament doesn't give an account of the planting of these churches. Paul may have had a hand in planting these churches during the years when he lived in Cilicia, prior to the time Barnabas sought him out to involve him in the work at Antioch.

Churches in both Syria and Cilicia are addressed in the letter from the Jerusalem Council. Silas may well have read that letter in these churches since he was one of the

Silas was one of the two prophets sent by the Jerusalem church to Antioch to convey the decision regarding how Gentiles are received into the church. Later in his ministry, Silas teamed with Peter on a mission in Pontus and Cappadocia. He served as Peter's scribe, writing 1 Peter and perhaps other letters.

19

designated representatives to communicate the decision of the Jerusalem Council.

THE CIRCUMCISION OF TIMOTHY (ACTS 16:1–3)

From Cilicia, Paul and Silas journeyed to Derbe. This had been Paul and Barnabas's last area of work on their first missionary journey. They traveled from Derbe to Lystra, home of Timothy, a young disciple who likely was converted as Paul preached in Lystra several years earlier.

Paul wanted to take Timothy as a companion along with Silas and himself. Before doing that, Paul insisted on circumcising Timothy, whose mother, Eunice, was Jewish and whose father was Greek. Sons of Jewish mothers were considered Jewish. Evidently Paul believed that an uncircumcised Jewish man—even though a Christian—would be a stumbling block to Jews.

"Do not neglect your gift, which was given you through a prophetic message when the body of elders laid their hands on you" (1 Tim. 4:14).

This may have been a occasion for Timothy being set apart for ministry. Luke says that Timothy was well respected not only by believers in Lystra but also by those from the neighboring city of Iconium. In his first letter to Timothy, Paul refers to an occasion when prophecy was made regarding Timothy's calling.

PAUL IN PHRYGIA AND GALATIA (ACTS 16:6)

Paul wanted to go next to the province of Asia. Somehow the Holy Spirit made known to Paul and Silas the fact that they should not go to Asia at this time. So they traveled through regions of Phrygia and Galatia. From there, they wanted to travel in a northerly direction to Bithynia but, once again, the Holy Spirit prevented them from going there.

PAUL IN TROAS (ACTS 16:6–11)

The only course left open now was to go westward. Thus Paul, Silas, and Timothy found themselves at Troas on the shore of the Aegean Sea. In Troas, Paul had a vision of a Macedonian man urging them to "come over to Macedonia and help us" (Acts 16:9). Paul and Silas interpreted this vision as a call from God to preach the gospel in the cities of Macedonia.

Paul, Timothy, and Silas boarded a ship and sailed to the island of Samothrace, where they spent a night. From there, they sailed to the port city of Macedonia, Neapolis. Next, they traveled by foot from Neapolis to Philippi along the Via Egnatia. At this point, Luke's narrative in Acts moves from third-person descriptions ("they") to first-person descriptions ("we"). Many interpreters believe that Luke joined Paul, Silas, and Timothy at this point in the journey.

The Conversion of Lydia (Acts 16:13–15). In Paul's first missionary journey, his practice when going to a city was first to preach the gospel in a synagogue. Evidently, there was no synagogue in Philippi. On the Sabbath, Paul and his companions went outside Philippi to the Gangites River where they expected to find people praying. There they found a number of women and began to speak with them. At least one of the women responded positively to Paul's message.

Lydia and her entire household were baptized. She then urged Paul and his companions to stay in her home during their time in Philippi.

The Servant Girl Healed (Acts 16:16–18). Once, as Paul and Silas were going to the place of prayer, they encountered a slave girl who told people's fortunes. She was being exploited by some men who were making money from her telling

The Via Egnatia was a strategic military highway that ran a distance of 500 miles across Macedonia to the Adriatic Sea.

Philippi

The seaport of Neapolis was the natural approach to the important city of Philippi, which lay only twelve miles away. This prosperous and strategic city was named after Philip II, king of Macedonia, the father of Alexander the Great. A strong Roman colony was established in this rich city.

"And a certain woman named Lydia, from the city of Thyatira, a seller of purple fabrics, a worshiper of God, was listening; and the Lord opened her heart to respond to the things spoken by Paul" (Acts 16:14, NASB).

fortunes. She announced that Paul and Silas were servants of God who were there to show the way of salvation. She continued her harassment of the apostles for many days. Finally Paul rebuked the spirit in the name of Jesus and it departed.

The men who were profiting financially from this became angry. They had lost their source of revenue. They apprehended Paul and Silas and brought them to the officials of the city. They charged the missionaries with teaching things that were unlawful. In the process of making the charges, they stirred up the crowd that was witnessing these proceedings.

Beaten and Imprisoned (Acts 16:19–24). The officials of Philippi tore Paul and Silas's clothes from them, had them beaten and thrown into jail where they were put into stocks in the inmost part of the jail. In the middle of the night, Paul and Silas prayed and sang aloud to God so that the other prisoners heard them.

The Earthquake and Conversion of the Jailer (Acts 16:25–34). While this was happening, there was an earthquake of such magnitude that the jail was shaken, the doors opened, and the prisoners released from their stocks. The commotion woke the jailer. When he saw what had happened, he assumed that all the prisoners had escaped and he would pay with his own life. So he drew his sword and was about to take his own life when Paul cried out to him, urging him not to fall on his sword. Paul assured him that all the prisoners were still in place. The jailer found a light and came to Paul and Silas asking what he must do to be saved. Paul told him to believe in the Lord Jesus Christ and he would be saved. He and his household listened as Paul set forth the gospel. They all believed and were baptized. The jailer washed the wounds they sustained from the beating the previous day. He also provided a meal for them.

It was illegal to flog a Roman citizen in public.

Paul and Silas Released; Depart from Philippi (Acts 16:35–40). The next day the officials of the city sent their policemen to release Paul and Silas. But Paul told the policemen to have the officials come themselves. He told the policemen to remind the officials that they had been beaten and jailed without a trial—not to mention the fact that they were Roman citizens. When the officials heard this, they were afraid and came to release Paul and Silas.

Before leaving Philippi, Paul and Silas went to the home of Lydia where they met with and encouraged the believers.

PAUL IN THESSALONICA (ACTS 17:1–9; 1 THESS. 2:9; 2 THESS. 3:6–10; PHIL. 4:16)

From Philippi, Paul and Silas traveled the Via Egnatia approximately 100 miles to Thessalonica. Enroute they traveled through Amphipolis and Appollonia.

Paul and Silas Preach in the Synagogue (Acts 17:1–4). For three successive Sabbath days Paul preached in the synagogue at Thessalonica and was successful in winning many Jews and Greeks to the Christian faith. This aroused the jealousy of the Jews.

Jason Brought Before the Magistrate (Acts 17:5–9). Several Jews gathered and "started a riot in the city" (v. 5). A man named Jason was Paul's host. The Jews attacked the house of Jason, thinking that Paul and Silas were there. They brought Jason and others before the authorities and charged them with being members of a

Thessalonica

Founded in 315 B.C., the city was named by a general of Alexander the great, Cassander. Having an excellent harbor, and located at the termination of a major trade route, it was one of the two most important commercial centers in Greece, along with Corinth. When Paul visited the city, it was larger than Philippi, which reflected a predominately Roman culture. The book of Acts testifies to the presence of a Jewish synagogue there (17:11).

23

dangerous sect. The ruler required bond of Jason and released the others.

It was now apparent that the people were so excited and opposition so strong that the disciples could not accomplish any more at Thessalonica. They had, however, established a strong church there. In fact, the church at Thessalonica became a model church for all of the believers throughout Macedonia and Achaia.

"For our gospel did not come to you in word only, but also in power and in the Holy Spirit and with full conviction. . . . And for this reason we also constantly thank God that when you received from us the word of God's message, you accepted it not as the word of men, but for what it really is, the word of God, which also performs its work in you who believe" (1 Thess. 1:5; 2:13, NASB).

No miracles are reported in connection with the founding of this church, but from Paul's first letter to them, it is evident that the Spirit was strongly at work taking the Word of God and making it of great effect among the Thessalonians. They were transformed from idolaters to become persons who served the living God.

The Faithfulness and Charity of the Thessalonians (1 Thess. 1:1–8; 2:13–16; 4:9–10). While Paul was in Thessalonica he supported himself by manual labor, which was a common practice with him. He was very sensitive about receiving any help from his friends, but he made an exception of the Philippian church, from which he received occasional help here (Phil. 4:16) and later in Corinth. To the selections given above from 1 Thessalonians should be added the passages in which Paul expresses his love for the disciples at Thessalonica (see 1 Thess. 3:7–13; 2 Thess. 1:2–7, 11–12; 2:13–17; 3:1–5).

PAUL IN BEREA (ACTS 17:10–14; 1 THESS. 2:17–20; 3:1–5)

Paul and Silas Preach in the Synagogue (Acts 17:10–13). With strong opposition against Paul and Silas aroused in Thessalonica, they were escorted out of the city at night and traveled on to Berea—about fifty miles southwest of Thessalonica. As was Paul's custom, his first went to the synagogue.

Luke describes the Bereans as more noble than the Thessalonians. They listened intently to Paul's case for Jesus as Messiah and they checked what he said against their Hebrew Scriptures. Many Jews and Greeks believed as did many prominent Greek women.

Meanwhile, in Thessalonica, the opposition to Paul and his message didn't die down. The Thessalonian rabble rousers heard Paul was in Berea. So they traveled to Berea and began to stir up opposition. Some of Paul's friends accompanied him out of the city and to the coast where they boarded a ship for Athens. Silas and Timothy continued in Berea. Paul sent word to Timothy to go back to Thessalonica to encourage the work that had been started (1 Thessalonians 3:1–2). Paul asked Timothy and Silas to join him later in Athens.

PAUL IN ATHENS (ACTS17:15–34; 1 THESS. 3:1–2)

Paul Debates with the Jews and the Greek Philosophers (Acts 17:16–21). The large number of idols in Athens was deeply offensive to Paul. This religious condition and its relationship to the God of Israel may have been a topic for discussion as he went to the synagogue. There he talked with both Jews and God-fearing Greeks. He also went to the famous marketplace where he engaged the Athenians in discussions of a philosophical and religious nature.

The Address on Mar's Hill and Its Effect (Acts 17:22–34). Representatives from two well-known Greek philosophical schools, Epicureans and Stoics, began to debate with Paul. They thought he was advocating a new and foreign

Athens

The city, which was probably named for the wisdom goddess Athene, was already an ancient place by the time Paul visited it. Athens was the home of three of the most influential philosphers in history: Socrates, Plato, and Aristotle. It became the scene of the world's first experiment with democratic government. It was destroyed by the Persians early in the fifth century B.C., but during the administration of Pericles the city was rebuilt into an architectural wonder.

" 'For in him we live and move and have our being.' As some of your own poets have said, 'We are his offspring'" (Acts 17:28). Paul quotes the Stoic poet Aratus.

Aeropagus

The Aeropagus was the site of Paul's speech to the Epicurean and Stoic philosophers of Athens, Greece. It was a rocky hill about 370 feet high, not far from the Acropolis and the Agora (marketplace). The word was also used to refer to the council that originally met on this hill. The name probably was derived from Ares, the Greek name for the god of war known to the Romans as Mars.

god, Anastasis (resurrection). Their curiosity was aroused, and so they invited Paul to their intellectual forum—the Areopagus.

Here on Mars Hill Paul delivered one of his most quoted sermons. As in Lystra, Paul was keenly sensitive to his audience. He began where they were and moved from there to present the gospel.

Luke mentions that a number of people believed Paul's message including Dionysius, a member of the Areopagus, and a woman, Damaris. Nothing is said of a church being planted in Athens at this time.

PAUL IN CORINTH (ACTS 18:1–2)
(Duration: Eighteen months)

From Athens, Paul traveled the fifty miles westward to Corinth. There he met a Jewish couple, Aquila and Priscilla, who had recently left Rome because of an edict of the Emperor Claudius. They, like Paul, were tentmakers and so he lived and worked with them. Aquila and Priscilla, who were already believers, would become two of Paul's strongest partners in the gospel.

In Corinth, Silas and Timothy rejoined Paul. They brought him good news from the young church in Thessalonica. And it was from Corinth that Paul wrote two letters (1, 2 Thessalonians) to encourage this church.

Paul spent Sabbaths in the Corinthian synagogue reasoning with both Jews and Greeks and preaching Jesus as Messiah. Eventually the opposition became so great, Paul left the synagogue and began meeting next door in the house of Titius Justus, a Gentile God-fearer. Also converted to faith in Christ was Crispus, the ruler of the synagogue, and all of his household. Crispus's witness resulted in many Corinthians believing and being baptized.

Paul's Vision (Acts 18:9–11). To encourage Paul amid growing opposition, God sent a vision at night assuring him of protection and guidance. He remained in Corinth for eighteen months, teaching and preaching the word of God.

Paul Before Gallio (Acts 18:12–18). With a change in Roman government, Gallio became the proconsul of the province. The Jews seized the opportunity for driving Paul out of the city. He was brought before Gallio where the Jews accused him of "persuading the people to worship God in ways contrary to the law" (v. 13). His accusers failed to convince Gallio, who refused to punish Paul.

FROM CORINTH TO ANTIOCH (ACTS 18:18–23)

Having been in Corinth for about two years, Paul took Priscilla and Aquila and began the journey back to Antioch. En route Paul visited the cities of Cenchrea and Ephesus, where he left Priscilla and Aquila. He spent a little time in the synagogue in Ephesus and promised to return if God willed. Paul then sailed from Ephesus eastward across the Mediterranean to Caesarea Maritima. From there he went to Jerusalem and then back to Antioch, the starting point for his first two missionary journeys.

The City of Corinth

The city of Corinth was one of the four prominent centers in the New Testament account of the church. Corinth was located on a narrow strip of land that connected the Peloponesian Peninsula with northern Greece. It had two seaports, Cenchrea on the Aegean side in the east and Lechaeum at the edge of the gulf of Corinth in the west. The city's location made it a crossroads for travel and commerce and contributed to its prosperity. Ship captains, eager to avoid the stormy dangers of sailing around the Peloponesian Straits on the south, would dock at one port of Corinth. Their cargo was unloaded, hauled overland, and then loaded in another vessel on the opposite side. They avoided the risk of losing ships and lives in the dangerous voyage along the southern route.

Rome destroyed Corinth in 146 B.C. but a century later it was rebuilt on the same location.

While Paul was away from Antioch, a Jew from Alexandria named Apollos came to Ephesus. Apollos had a thorough knowledge of the Scriptures and was accurate and forceful in his preaching Jesus. However, he lacked a full understanding of the way of God, so Priscilla and Aquila took him aside and instructed him. Apollos became even more successful in his ministry. He greatly strengthened believers by using the Scriptures to demonstrate that Jesus was the Christ. After this he became a preacher of the gospel, first in Achaia, and then in Corinth (Acts 18:27; 19:1).

There is no evidence in the New Testament that Apollos and Paul ever viewed each other as rivals. Some New Testament references compare Apollos with Paul or Peter (1 Cor.1:12; 3:4–6, 22). In 1 Corinthians 4:6, Paul placed Apollos on the same level as himself. He also referred to Apollos as his brother (16:12).

PAUL'S THIRD MISSIONARY JOURNEY (A.D. 54–58) (ACTS 18:23–21:16)

(Duration: Four years)

After Paul spent some time in Antioch, he began this third missionary journey by going through the regions of Galatia and Phrygia (Acts 18:22–23) in order to strengthen and encourage the churches that had been planted there. His aim was to return to Ephesus where he had left Priscilla and Aquila and had promised those in the synagogue that he would be back.

THE WORK OF APOLLOS IN EPHESUS (ACTS 18:24–28)

In this city of rhetoricians and sophists, the erudition and eloquent speaking of Apollos were contrasted with the unlearned simplicity with which Paul had studiously presented the gospel to his Corinthian hearers. Thus many attached themselves to the new teacher, and called themselves by the name of Apollos, while others formed themselves as the party of Paul (1 Cor. 1:12), forgetting that Christ could not be "divided," and that Paul and Apollos were merely ministers through whom they had believed (1 Cor. 3:5).

PAUL IN EPHESUS (ACTS 19:1–20:35; 1 COR. 1:1, 8–11; 4:11–12, 17; 16:3–11, 15–19; 2 COR. 13:2)

(Duration: Three years)

Paul Arrives in Ephesus (Acts 19:1–7). For nearly three years Paul lived and worked in Ephesus, the capital of Asia. This was his longest ministry in one place, and this great city with its strategic situation and leadership furnished Paul an opportunity for the use of all his facilities as a preacher of the gospel and as a Christian statesman.

When he first arrived, Paul discovered some twelve disciples who had been baptized with John (the Baptist's) baptism alone and not with the Holy Spirit. Paul told them the relationship between John the Baptist and Jesus. They were then baptized in the name of Jesus and received the Holy Spirit.

Paul in the Synagogue and School of Tyrannus (Acts 19:8–12). Before Paul left Priscilla and Aquila in Ephesus on his return to Judea, he promised to come back to the synagogue in Ephesus if it were God's will. Now Paul delivered on that promise. For three months he spoke boldly about the kingdom of God to those gathered at the synagogue. Resistance arose and with it a lot of negative publicity about the Christian way. So Paul changed locations. He moved from the synagogue to the lecture hall of Tyrannus.

Luke says that Paul taught in this setting for two years. This teaching reached far beyond Ephesus proper. Those converted and nurtured during this time carried the gospel throughout the province of Asia to both Jews and Gentiles. This may well have been the time that churches were planted in Colosse, Hieropolis, Sardis, Philadelphia, Laodicea, Thyatira, and Pergamum.

The Defeat of the Jewish Exorcists (Acts 19:13–30). Paul not only taught with power. God worked miracles through him. Seven sons of Sceva, a Jewish chief priest, apparently witnessed some of the miracles Paul did in the name of Jesus and they attempted to do the

City of Ephesus

The ancient city of Ephesus was located in western Asia Minor at the mouth of the Cayster River and was an important seaport. Situated between the Maeander River to the south and the Hermus River to the north, Ephesus had excellent access to both river valleys, which allowed it to flourish as a commercial center. Due to the accumulation of silt deposited by the river, the present site of the city is approximately five to six miles inland. Under the Romans, Ephesus thrived, reaching the pinnacle of its greatness during the first and second centuries of the Christian area. At the time of Paul, Ephesus was probably the fourth largest city in the world, with a population estimated at 250,000.

same. In one case, they attempted to cast a demon out of a man by invoking "the name of Jesus, whom Paul preaches." The demon spoke to them saying that it knew Jesus and Paul but it didn't know them. The possessed man attacked and beat them so that they left the house naked and badly hurt.

This passage gives an interesting account of the miracles Paul was able to work at Ephesus. Ephesus was the home of Eastern magic and claimed to avert misfortune by the use of magic charms and incantations. Paul's use of miracles labeled him as a "magic" person in the eyes of the people. Although a misrepresentation of Paul's work, it received the attention and devotion of many, who burned their books on magic.

A drachma was roughly equivalent to a day's wages. So several million dollars worth of books went up in smoke as the gospel did its work in the Ephesians' hearts.

This event evoked awe and fear in Ephesus. The name of Jesus was held in high esteem among them and people came forth to bring to light their evil deeds. Those who had practiced the black arts brought their books of magic and sorcery out and burned them publicly. The value of these books was 50,000 drachmas.

Paul Plans to Go Through Macedonia and Achaia, then Jerusalem and Rome (Acts 19:21; 1 Cor. 16:3–7). Paul next proposed to go to Jerusalem. He intended to go by way of Macedonia and Achaia. This would give him the opportunity to visit the churches he, Silas, and Timothy had planted on his second missionary journey: Philippi, Thessalonica, Berea, and Corinth. Paul sent Timothy and Erastus ahead of him to the Macedonian churches. From Jerusalem he hoped to sail to Rome.

"But I shall come to you after I go through Macedonia, for I am going through Macedonia; and perhaps I shall stay with you, or even spend the winter, that you may send me on my way wherever I may go"
(1 Cor. 16:5–6, NASB).

Demetrius the Silversmith Creates an Uproar Against Paul (Acts 19:22–41). An insurrection, led by Demetrius the silversmith, made it necessary for Paul to leave Ephesus sooner than he had wanted. Paul left immediately for Troas, but was so far ahead of schedule that he had to wait some time for Titus's return. Finally, he decided not to wait, and pressed onward to Macedonia. Paul traveled to Greece from Macedonia and stayed in Corinth for three months. His intention was to sail back to Syria from Greece but while there, he learned of a plot on his life. He, therefore, retraced his steps back through Macedonia on his way to Troas. Luke mentions a number of men who accompanied Paul on this journey.

Paul Preaches Throughout Macedonia (Acts 20:1–2; 2 Cor. 8:1–5). Paul preached to many churches in Macedonia. The Macedonian Christians gave generously for the relief of the Jerusalem church. Paul emphasizes two characteristics of these believers: (1) their extreme poverty; and (2) their extreme generosity.

In Troas (Acts 20:7–12). Paul's traveling companions preceded him to Troas where he spent a week with the believers. On Sunday, the church was sharing a fellowship meal. Knowing that he would depart the next day, Paul spoke to the church. His message continued on into the night. One of the young men, Eutychus, fell asleep and fell out of the third story window he was sitting in. The believers feared he was dead. Paul stooped down and embraced and found that the boy was still alive. Those who saw this felt profound relief at his being alive. Paul continued to talk with the believers and shared another meal with them until daybreak when he departed.

PAUL'S JOURNEY TO JERUSALEM (ACTS 20:13–38; 21:1–11)

Paul Departs Troas (Acts 20:13–12). Luke and Paul's companions boarded a ship in Troas and

While in Greece Paul wrote his great epistle to the Romans and planned his trip to Spain (Acts 20:1–3; 2 Cor. 2:1; 9:3–4; 12:14; 13:1–3; Rom. 1:8–16; 15:22–29; 16:1–2, 21–23). The passage from Romans mentions Paul's companions in Corinth. These include Phoebe, who was a deaconess of the church at Cenchrea, the eastern port of Corinth. Nothing is known of her besides this. She was evidently the bearer of the epistle to the Romans. Timothy was a joint writer of Romans. Tertius was the *amanuensis* ("scribe") to whom Paul dictated the epistle.

"He was accompanied by Sopater son of Pyrrhus from Berea, Aristarchus and Secundus from Thessalonica, Gaius from Derbe, Timothy also, and Tychicus and Trophimus from the province of Asia" (Acts 20:4).

sailed for Assos where Paul would join them. He chose to travel by land from Troas to Assos. At Assos, Paul rejoined his companions and they sailed for Miletus. Paul wanted to reach Jerusalem by Pentecost and therefore decided not to go to Ephesus. Rather he sent word for the elders from Ephesus to join him in Miletus.

Paul had given focused attention to the church at Ephesus. He spent three years with them, no doubt realizing the strategic importance of that church for the work of Christ throughout Asia. Paul told them that he would likely never see them again and wanted to spend this time with them before he departed for Jerusalem.

James Stalker says there are two monuments to Paul's work in Ephesus. The first are the churches of Asia Minor addressed in John's Revelation. The second is Paul's letter to the Ephesians. Stalker says "this is perhaps the profoundest book in existence; yet its author evidently expected the Ephesians to understand it." Here is a book which "sounds the lowest depths of Christian doctrine and scales the loftiest heights of Christian experience....[It] is a testimony to the proficiency which Paul's converts had attained under his preaching in the capital of Asia" (James Stalker, *Life of St. Paul*, [Fleming H. Revell Company, 1950], 89).

"And when he had said these things, he knelt down and prayed with them all. And they began to weep aloud and embraced Paul, and repeatedly kissed him, grieving especially over the word which he had spoken, that they should see his face no more. And they were accompanying him to the ship" (Acts 20:36–38, NASB).

Paul's Fifth Visit to Jerusalem (21:7–16). Two final legs of his journey—Miletus to Tyre (Acts 21:1–6) and Ptolemias and Caesarea (Acts 21:7–11)—bring Paul to Jerusalem for the fifth time. At Tyre, several believers met him with a warning of what lay ahead at Jerusalem. From Caesarea, Paul departed for Jerusalem with several other Christians.

PAUL'S PRISON YEARS

PAUL IN JERUSALEM (ACTS 21:17–20)

Paul had hoped to reach Jerusalem by the time of the annual observance of the Passover feast. When he and his party finally arrived, it was fifty days later and the eve of the Day of Pentecost. Paul, Luke, and Trophimus made a formal call to James, the leader of the church at Jerusalem. Paul reported at length what God had done among the Gentiles, and all were deeply impressed and glorified God.

PAUL ATTEMPTS TO AVOID TROUBLE (ACTS 21:20–26)

However, James and the others who received this report were concerned about Paul's presence in Jerusalem. The rumor was that Paul had gone far beyond the agreement made at the Jerusalem conference. Jewish believers were saying that Paul was encouraging Jewish Christians to abandon the Law of Moses and to stop circumcising their sons. In order to stop this rumor, the brothers in Jerusalem made the following proposal to Paul.

They recommended that Paul join four men who were about to go through a ritual of purification. They believed that if Jewish Christians saw Paul participating in this ritual that he must not have abandoned Jewish traditions. Paul agreed to do this. He annouced the day on which this ritual would be complete and he would offer sacrifices in the Temple.

As the period of purification drew to a close, some Jews from Asia saw Paul in the Temple. They incited a riot by telling the crowds that Paul was turning people away from Jewish ways and that he had even defiled the Temple by bringing Gentiles into it. Earlier in the week these Jews from Asia had seen Paul with Trophimus, a Gentile Christian from Ephesus.

PAUL SEIZED IN THE TEMPLE (ACTS 21:27–39; 26:19–21)

The crowd seized Paul, took him out of the Temple, and would have killed him if the Roman commander of the cohort stationed at Antonia Fortress hadn't intervened and taken Paul into their custody. Paul asked the commander for permission to address the crowd.

Paul's Speech on the Barracks' Stairs (Acts 21:40–22:21–29). Paul spoke in Aramaic and gave a brief sketch of who he was and how he had been changed from a persecutor of Christians to a Christian himself. Paul told how the Lord had appeared to him in Jerusalem several years after his conversion. The Lord told him to leave Jerusalem—that he was being sent to the Gentiles.

When the crowd heard the word *Gentile*, they yelled in unison for Paul's death. He was unable to get their attention again so the commander took him into the barracks and was going to have him beaten in order to force the truth out of him. At this point, Paul let it be known that was a Roman citizen and couldn't be beaten without a trial.

PAUL'S SPEECH BEFORE THE SANHEDRIN (ACTS 22:30–23:9)

The Jews had Paul brought before the council without a charge. He knew this group and knew well enough that he did not have much chance before them. He ventured the statement that he had lived before God in all good conscience.

The high priest, Ananias, ordered one who stood by to smite Paul on the mouth. This unpardonable insult angered Paul and he bitterly denounced Ananias. For this he apologized, since he did not really know at the time that Ananias was the high priest.

At this point Paul did a thing for which he has sometimes been criticized. He knew that the council was part Pharisees and part Sadducees and that they were bitter enemies. He then cried out, "My brothers, I am a Pharisee, a son of a Pharisee." There immediately arose such a discussion and clamor between these two groups that the session could not be held. The chief captain, fearing that Paul would be harmed, ordered the soldiers to rescue him from the warring members and bring him into the castle. Again he had escaped death.

PAUL IN THE BARRACKS (ACTS 23:10–11)

Paul was still held as a prisoner and the following night received a visitation of the Lord who said to him, "Take courage! As you have testified about me in Jerusalem, so you must also testify in Rome" (v. 11). He needed this assurance. He could now be assured that he would be spared to get to Rome though he little knew how long it would take or in what way this was to occur.

THE JEWS PLOT TO KILL PAUL (ACTS 23:12–33)

The Plot and Its Discovery (Acts 23:12–22). These Jews having been outwitted by Paul in the Sanhedrin were now desperately determined to kill him. They bound themselves under a curse, saying that they would neither eat nor drink till they had killed Paul. These forty desperate men then informed the council of their vow, asked

Ananias the High Priest

Ananias was the high priest of the Jewish court known as the Sanhedrin. This is the court that tried Paul in Acts 23. As was typical of high priests who belonged to the aristocratic Jewish group known as the Sadducees, he was quite concerned to appease Roman authorities and representatives. This desire may have prompted Ananias to take such a personal interest in the case of Paul, especially since some Roman authorities suspected the apostle of sedition against Rome.

Because of Ananias's pro-Roman sentiments, he was assassinated by anti-Roman Jewish revolutionaries at the outbreak of the first great Jewish revolt against Rome in A.D. 66.

them to request another trial "on the pretext of wanting more accurate information about his case." Their plot was to slay Paul as he was being transported to the trial.

The Plan of Escape (Acts 23:23–33). Paul's life was spared by another unexpected intervention. Luke tells in graphic style how Paul's nephew, the son of his sister, heard of this plot and then reported it to him, and how he asked one of the centurions to bring the boy to the chief captain. The lad then told of the plot, and the chief captain charged the boy not to tell anyone else. He then ordered two hundred soldiers, two hundred spearmen and seventy horsemen to take Paul that night to Caesarea. He sent a letter explaining the case to Felix at Caesarea. Upon his arrival in Caesarea, Paul was received by Felix and was placed in Herod's palace.

PAUL IN CAESAREA (ACTS 23:31–26:32)

(Duration: Two years, A.D. 58–60)

PAUL'S CONFINEMENT (ACTS 23:31–35)

Herod's judgment hall was in a palace at Caesarea and was occupied as the residence of the Roman procurator. Paul was confined in some apartment of this building.

PAUL BEFORE FELIX (ACTS 24:1–23)

The Argument of Tertullus (Acts 24:1–9). Paul's accusers, who turned out to be not the Asian Jews, but Jews from Jerusalem, came to Caesarea for the trial. They were led by a Roman lawyer, Tertullus, whom they had employed. Tertullus began his address with profuse praise of Felix and then made his charges against Paul, which were threefold:

1. *Sedition.* Tertullus charged Paul with being a pest in the community, a disturber of the peace, one who incited Jews across the Empire to rebellion against Rome.

2. *Heresy.* The next count in the indictment was heresy, being a ringleader in the sect whom he contemptuously called the Nazarenes—a term of reproach, which had been often applied to the followers of Christ.

3. *Sacrilege.* The last charge was profaning the Temple—a serious charge, but utterly unfounded.

Paul's Reply (Acts 24:10–21). Paul had no lawyer, but with skill he presented his own case. He disproved the charge that he had profaned the Temple. He then admitted freely that he was a

The procurator at Caesarea at this time was Antonius Felix. He was a freedman who obtained his office by political favor, was disdained by other officials and was despised by the Jews. His term of office was one of faulty administration, turmoil and terror. He was finally recalled by Nero in A.D. 59.

"A few days later Felix came with his wife, Drusilla, who was Jewish. Sending for Paul, they listened as he told them about faith in Christ Jesus. As he reasoned with them about righteousness and self-control and the judgment to come, Felix was terrified. 'Go away for now,' he replied. 'When it is more convenient, I'll call for you again'" (Acts 24:24, NLT).

Nero appointed Porcius Festus to replace Felix in A.D. 60. He served as procurator of Judea until his death in A.D. 62.

Christian and insisted that this was the "true Judaism." Paul won his case and should have been released.

Felix Suspends Judgment (Acts 24:22–23). Felix should have declared Paul free and immediately released him, but his fear of the Jewish leaders caused him to postpone his decision and keep Paul in prison.

THE TRIAL BEFORE FESTUS AND PAUL'S APPEAL TO CAESAR (ACTS 25:1–12; 28:17–19).

When Festus came to Caesarea to succeed Felix, one of his first acts was to go to Jerusalem and meet with the Jewish leaders. They hadn't forgotten the case against Paul and so in their conversations with Festus, they brought the matter up.

They wanted Paul brought to Jerusalem to stand trial. Festus told them that if they wanted to bring charges against Paul, they could come to Caesarea and do so. Over a week later, Festus returned to Caesarea along with the leaders from Jerusalem. Again, they brought charges against Paul but were not able to bring evidence to support their claims. Paul denied having violated Jewish or Roman law or desecrating the Temple.

Since Festus was unacquainted with these matters, he suggested that the case be referred to the Sanhedrin in Jerusalem with himself as assessor. Paul knew what this would mean; he would have no chance before this tribunal in Jerusalem. He would never consent to this arrangement. He was a Roman citizen and had the right to enter a protest and appeal the case to the Emperor. He, therefore, cried, "I appeal to Caesar." This unexpected development took Festus by surprise, but he knew it was a valid appeal.

So he had to give his judgment: "You have appealed to Caesar. To Caesar you will go!"

PAUL AND AGRIPPA (ACTS 25:13–26:32)

Festus's Preliminary Conference with Agrippa (25:13–22). Several days later, King Agrippa II and Bernice came to Caesarea to visit Festus. Festus told Agrippa about Paul's case and shared his perplexity in how best to handle the case. Festus confessed that he could see no valid charges against Paul but since Paul appealed to Caesar, he was going to have to send him to Rome. Festus knew he would have to specify charges against Paul as he sent them to Caesar and so he asked King Agrippa's counsel in crafting a letter to Caesar.

Paul Appears Before Agrippa and Bernice (25:23–27). A state occasion of great pomp was arranged and Paul was brought in to speak before the assembly, presided over by Agrippa.

Paul's Defense (26:1–31). Paul presented his case. His address was long and persuasive. He reviewed his experiences and then preached Jesus Christ with a view to winning the governor to Christ. Festus, Agrippa, and the others apparently were moved by the eloquent words of Paul. But they made no decision. After Paul was dismissed, Agrippa and Festus conferred, and they privately agreed that Paul had done nothing worthy of death. But he could not be released because he had appealed to Caesar.

Herod Agrippa II

Herod was the name given to the family ruling Palestine immediately before and to some degree during the first half of the first Christian century. Herod Agrippa II governed northern and eastern Palestine. He was the last of the Herodian dynasty. Bernice was both his sister and his mistress.

"Agrippa interrupted him. 'Do you think you can make me a Christian so quickly?' Paul replied, 'Whether quickly or not, I pray to God that both you and everyone here in this audience might become the same as I am, except for these chains'" (Acts 26:28–29, NLT).

Paul's Journey to Rome

Note the appearance again of the "we" sections of Acts. Luke, the author of Acts, joined Paul for this trip to Rome and remained with him until Paul was delivered to the custody of soldiers in Rome (28:16). The journey to Rome involved typical navigational practices and patterns of the first century. Due to dangerous weather conditions, no sailing occurred in the Mediterranean Sea during the period from mid-November to early March. Paul's voyage was near the beginning of this dangerous period.

PAUL'S JOURNEY FROM CAESAREA TO ROME (ACTS 27:1–28:16)

(A.D. Autumn 60–Spring 61)

PAUL, LUKE, AND ARISTARCHUS SAIL TO CRETE (ACTS 27:1–13)

Luke was with Paul and describes with great vividness their experiences on the way to Rome. He writes in the first person plural and gives a wealth of detail which is of great value, not only to those interested in Paul's work, but to all who are interested in nautical life in the First Century.

Paul and a number of other prisoners were placed in the hands of Julius of the Augustan band for the journey. It would be necessary to use several ships for the voyage, transferring at several ports. They made "slow headway" on this ship for many days and finally, with great difficulty, they came to a little port on the southern shore of Crete, called Fair Havens.

Because of the winter storms travel on the sea was extremely hazardous from early November till early in February. The crew of the ship did not want to spend the winter at Fair Havens but were anxious to get to the better harbor of Phoenix, about fifty miles west. The crew held a meeting to decide what should be done. Paul, an experienced sea traveler, was invited to the council where he argued against the proposal that they slip out of the harbor of Fair Havens, stay close to shore and try to get into Phoenix for the winter. Julius, however, approved the plan, being tempted by the good prospects "when a gentle south wind began to blow" (27:13).

THE STORM (ACTS 27:14–38)

Luke's description of the storm and subsequent shipwreck are classic. A hurricane-force wind called a "northeaster" swept down the island. The ship was caught in this wind and could not maneuver. The storm raged for fourteen days. Hungry and weary, the crew lost hope of being saved.

THE SHIPWRECK AND THE ESCAPE TO LAND (ACTS 27:39–44)

Luke gives in detail and with precision the steps taken by which the lives of all were saved in the most remarkable record of a shipwreck in existence and the most imposing account of ancient ships. When every means had been employed to save the ship and it appeared altogether hopeless Paul received a visit from an angel who assured him that all would be spared. Paul soon came to be the leading figure on the ship. He saved the prisoners from the trickery of the soldiers. At last the ship went to pieces on the rocks but every life on board was spared.

PAUL IN MELITA (ACTS 28:1–10)

(Duration: Three months)

The Islanders (Acts 28:1–2). The land on which they came was the island of Melita (Malta). They were received with kindness by the inhabitants of the island who built a fire by which they could warm themselves.

Paul's Miracles (Acts 28:3–10). As Paul assisted the natives in gathering wood for the fire he was bitten by a poisonous viper. To the amazement of all the islanders he suffered no ill effects from the bite and the people came to look upon him as a god. Publius, the chief man of the island, received and entertained

Paul and Luke courteously for three days. The father of Publius was sick from a "fever and dysentery," and Paul healed him. This was the beginning of a fruitful ministry of healing and teaching on the island.

JOURNEY FROM MELITA TO ROME (ACTS 28:11–15)

The Three Taverns was about 35 miles from Rome.

With the arrival of spring a ship bound for Rome was ready to sail. On this ship the last leg of the sea voyage was made. They spent three days in Syracuse (Sicily), one day at Rhegium and after two more days sailing, arrived at Puteoli. Evidently Paul had been able to send word of the arrival of the ship to the Christians at Rome for they were met before they reached the city by brethren who came to greet Paul at the Forum of Appius and the Three Taverns. Luke says when Paul saw the brethren, he thanked God and took courage.

PAUL'S FIRST ROMAN CAPTIVITY

(Duration: Two years, A.D. 61–63)

PAUL'S FIRST ROMAN CAPTIVITY ACCORDING TO ACTS (28:16–31)

After the long and tempestuous journey from Caesarea, Julius brought his prisoners at last to Rome. Upon arriving in the city, he took all these except Paul to the prisoner's quarters on the Caelian Hill and turned them over to the commander. For some reason, possibly because of the letter of Festus, or more probable, the good behavior of Paul on the journey, he was given special privileges. He was allowed to live outside the prisoner's quarters, apparently in the home of some Christian. He was by no means free since he was chained to a guard at all times. He could receive friends and certainly Luke and Aristarchus were allowed to visit him freely.

Paul Meets the Chief Jews of Rome (Acts 28:16–29).

1. *The First Meeting (Acts 28:16–22).* After resting three days, Paul called together the chief Jews, as his custom was, and reported to them fully concerning his situation, the charges against him, and the reason for his appeal to Caesar. These Jewish leaders assured Paul that they had received no letter from Judea concerning him. They expressed their desire to hear him fully concerning this "sect," the Christians.

2. *The Second Meeting* (Acts 28:23–29). Accordingly, a date was set for all the Jews of Rome who were interested to come to Paul's lodging. On the appointed day, the second meeting took place, and a very large number gathered to hear

him expound his faith in Christ. From morning until evening he explained the scriptural testimonies to Jesus as Messiah. Some were persuaded to believe; others rejected his words and they fell into a bitter controversy among themselves. When Paul saw how bitterly they opposed his message, he announced that henceforth he should leave the Jews alone and devote himself to winning the Gentiles in Rome (v. 28).

3. *Paul Lives Two Years in House Arrest (Acts 28:16, 30–31).* During this first captivity, it is certain that Paul had great freedom. For two years he rented his own quarters and was able to receive those who came to see him. He was free to preach and teach.

According to Roman custom he was bound by the hand to the soldier who guarded him, and was never left alone day or night. As the soldiers would relieve guards in constant succession, the praetorians one by one were brought into communication with the "prisoner of Jesus Christ," and thus he was able to affirm that his bonds had borne witness to the gospel "throughout the imperial regiments" (Phil. 1:13).

PAUL'S FIRST ROMAN CAPTIVITY ACCORDING TO PHILEMON, COLOSSIANS, EPHESIANS, AND PHILIPPIANS

Paul Is a Prisoner (Philem. 1; 8; 9; Col. 4:3, 18; Eph. 3:1; 4:1; 6:18–20; Phil. 1:7, 12–14, 16). Upon his arrival in Rome he was delivered over to the commander of the imperial guards, the prefect of the praetorians, under whose charge he appears to have remained throughout his captivity. He represented himself as strictly a prisoner and spoke often of his bonds. At times he used more precise language, mentioning the "coupling chain" (Acts 28:20; Eph. 6:20).

Paul's Expectation of Release (Phil. 1:23–27; 2:24; Philem. 22). It is clear from these passages that Paul fully expected to be released and to continue his ministry. He asked Philemon to prepare him a place of lodging, and expressed his desire to soon visit the Philippian believers.

Paul's Companions. The epistles reveal that Paul met with many companions during his captivity in Rome.

1. *Timothy* (Philem. 1; Col. 1:1; Phil. 1:1; 2:19–23). Paul's faithful companion and coworker in the gospel.

2. *Epaphras* (Philem. 23; Col. 1:3–8; 4:12–13). Epaphras was an evangelist who founded the church at Colosse and continued from time to time to work there, "always laboring earnestly for you in his prayers, that you may stand perfect and fully assured in all the will of God" (Col. 4:12, NASB.)

3. *Onesimus* and *Tychicus* (Philem. 10–21; Col. 4:7–9; Eph. 6:21–22). *Onesimus,* the runaway slave, likely had sought the metropolis as a convenient hiding place, where he might escape detection among its crowds and make a livelihood as best he could. To aid the slave, Paul avails himself of the services of *Tychicus,* who was probably an Ephesian, and was one of those who left Greece with him for Jerusalem (Acts 20:4). He is made the bearer of the epistle to the Colossians (Col. 4:7–8), and at the same time Paul sends with him Onesimus (Col. 4:9).

4. *Marcus, Aristarchus, Demas, Luke, Jesus (Justus)* (Philem. 24; Col. 4:10–11, 14). *Marcus,* doubtless John Mark, who had been associated with St. Paul in his earlier missionary work (Acts 12:25; 15:37). *Arisiarchus,* the Thessalonian. He had started with Paul on his voyage from Jerusalem to Rome, but probably had parted from the apostle at Myra. If so, he must have rejoined him at Rome at a later date. He would be well known in proconsular Asia, which he had visited from time to time (Acts 19:29; 20:4; 27:2). How was he Paul's "fellow-prisoner"? The most

probable solution would he that his relations with Paul in Rome excited suspicion and led to a temporary confinement. *Demas* afterwards deserted Paul, "having loved this present world" (2 Tim. 4:10, KJV). He is named with *Luke*, who remained faithful to the end (2 Tim. 4:11). *Jesus*, called *Justus*, probably was not a man of any prominence in the church, but his personal devotion to the apostle prompted this honorable mention.

5. *Ephaphroditus* (Phil. 2:25–30; 4:18, 22). Brings a gift from the Philippians and is made the bearer of the letter to the Philippians.

Between the First and Second Roman Captivities A.D. 63–67

(Duration: Four or five years)

Luke's account of Paul first imprisonment in Rome closes on a positive but inconclusive note. We are not told of the outcome of his appeal to Caesar—the reason he was taken to Rome.

There is a strong tradition that Paul was released from his first imprisonment around A.D. 63. What is known of Paul following two years into his first imprisonment in Rome has to be pieced together from his Prison Epistles (Ephesians, Colossians, Philippians, Philemon) and the Pastoral Epistles (1, 2 Timothy, Titus).

Many traditional interpreters view the Prison Epistles as being written during Paul's first imprisonment. First Timothy and Titus are thought to have been written between Paul's two imprisonments and 2 Timothy written shortly before Paul's death during a brief second imprisonment.

In what follows, we will look at the evidence in these letters that is suggestive of what Paul did beyond what Luke tells us in Acts.

PAUL'S CONJECTURAL TRAVELS ACCORDING TO ROMANS, PHILEMON, COLOSSIANS, PHILIPPIANS

There are several passages which simply express a wish or an intention of Paul to make certain journeys at some future time. These allusions are taken from Romans, Philemon, Colossians, and Philippians.

"For the next two years, Paul lived in his own rented house. He welcomed all who visited him, proclaiming the Kingdom of God with all boldness and teaching about the Lord Jesus Christ. And no one tried to stop him" (Acts 28:30–31, NLT).

Philippi

Paul's favorite church in Macedonia was at Philippi. After his visit there on his second missionary journey (Acts 16:12) he went to Macedonia twice before he was imprisoned in Rome (Acts 20:1, 6), and during the second of these visits he stopped at Philippi. The only reason for supposing that he went there again, after his release from prison, is his well-known affection for the Philippian church and his expressed desire and intention of coming to them again in Philippians 1:26; 2:24.

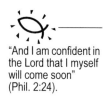

"And I am confident in the Lord that I myself will come soon" (Phil. 2:24).

Colosse

Paul's Desire to Visit Colossae (Philem. 22). Paul's visit to Colossae is placed after his release from prison. In his letter to Philemon, who lived at Colossae, he requested his friend to prepare him a lodging (v. 22). This shows Paul's desire to visit Colosse, but whether he ever followed out his plan or not cannot be decided.

The Personnel at the Church at Colossae (Col. 4:12, 17; Philem. 1–2, 10–11). Among those at Colosse, Paul mentions Epaphras, Philemon, Apphia, Archippus, and Onesimus. Epaphras, the founder of the church in Colosse, may have been there, having been liberated from prison in Rome at the same time with the apostle. The letter to Philemon introduces the reader to an ordinary household in a small town in Phrygia. Philemon was head of the household. Apphia seems to be the wife of Philemon, and Archippus was a son of Philemon and Apphia. The slave of this household was Onesimus, the runaway, who was converted under Paul at Rome and later restored to his owner, Philemon.

Laodicea and Hierapolis

Paul's Care for the Churches of Laodicea and Hierapolis (Col. 2:1; 4:12–13). The same reasons for deciding that Paul had not visited Colosse when he wrote Colossians hold good concerning Laodicea and Hierapolis. It is uncertain whether he visited those two towns after his imprisonment. If Paul had visited Colosse, he no doubt would have visited Laodicea and Hierapolis also.

The Personnel at the Church at Laodicea (Col. 4:15). Paul mentions one prominent member of the church in Laodicea—Nymphas. A portion of the group of believers at Laodicea, for unknown reasons, met for worship in the house of Nymphas.

The Connection of the Letter to the Colossians with the Laodiceans (Col. 4:16). The epistle to the Colossians was also intended for the church at Laodicea.

Paul's Letter to the Laodicean Church (Col. 4:16). Also, it is thought by some scholars that a letter to the Laodiceans from Paul has been lost. The "letter from Laodicea" may have been a circular letter to the Asiatic churches, sent to Laodicea as one the great centers.

Other Travels

If Paul traveled to Spain, he likely stopped in Crete upon his return. There he, Timothy, and Titus went across the island on a preaching tour. After a time Paul left Titus on Crete to continue the work begun there. He, Timothy, and Trophimus sailed to Miletus enroute to Ephesus. Paul left Trophimus ill at Miletus. In Ephesus, Paul found the churches' health threatened by false teaching. He left Timothy in Ephesus to take corrective action and headed to Troas. There he left his coat and some manuscripts with Carpus. From Troas, Paul sailed to Macedonia. During this time, he wrote to encourage both Timothy in Ephesus and Titus in Crete. Paul told Titus to come and join him in Nicopolis where he intended to spend the winter.

Spain

Paul expressed the intention of going to Spain (Rom. 15:24, 28; 2 Cor. 10:16). Sources outside the Bible like 1 Clement, The Acts of Peter, and the Muratorian Canon all support the claim that Paul did work in Spain.

During Paul's first imprisonment, he expected to go back to Macedonia and more specifically to Philippi (Phil. 1:26; 2:24).

ARREST AND SECOND IMPRISONMENT

Not long after Paul's release from his first imprisonment, Rome burned. On a summer night in A.D. 64, the fire started near the Circus Maximus and burned for six nights and seven days. Rumors began to circulate that the Emperor Nero himself was the instigator of the fire. As fingers began to point at Nero, he looked for a culprit and found it in the Christians.

As early as A.D. 65, the persecution was well under way. The Roman historian, Tacitus, says that those who confessed to be Christians were arrested and many of them were sentenced to death—not for setting the fire but for hatred of the human race. Tacitus describes in some detail the methods of execution.

Paul was likely arrested in the context of this widespread persecution. From his letter to Titus, we know that he anticipated seeing Titus in Nicopolis where he proposed to spend the winter. Some scholars believe Paul was arrested in Macedonia or Nicopolis or somewhere in between.

In any case, Paul was arrested and imprisoned a second time. This imprisonment did not allow the freedom of the first imprisonment. The persecution initiated by Nero had radically changed the climate of Rome as regards Christianity. Now, Paul is not only chained, but treated "like a criminal" (2 Tim. 2:9). His friends still visit him in his confinement, but we hear nothing of his preaching, It is dangerous and difficult (2 Tim. 1:16) to seek his prison, so perilous to show any public sympathy with him that no Christian ventures to stand by him in the court of justice (2 Tim. 4:16). Onesiphorus, a brother from Ephesus heard of Paul's imprisonment but had difficulty finding him.

Tacitus was not at all sympathetic with the Christians, but he made the following observation: "Hence, in spite of a guilt which had earned the most exemplary punishment, there arose a feeling of pity, because it was felt that they were being sacrificed not for the common good but to gratify the savagery of one man" (*Annals,* XV, 44).

Others believe that Paul, hearing of the escalating persecution in Rome, went to Rome voluntarily to be with his fellow Christians. The Acts of Paul, an apocryphal document from the late second century, says that Paul did go to Rome, where he was greeted at the gates of the city by Luke and Titus.

PAUL'S LONELINESS

The Absence of Friends (2 Tim. 1:15; 4:10, 12, 19, 20). Almost all of Paul's old friends are away from him now. But this was not all. Demas, who was present among Paul's friends in the first captivity, now forsakes the apostle, because he "loved this world," and had gone to Thessalonica. Add to this many of those in Asia who turned away from the apostle's teaching.

His Companions (2 Tim. 1:16–18; 4:11, 19, 21). Of his old companions, Luke alone is with him. No mention has been made of him since he was with Paul in the first imprisonment; it is not known whether he was with him during his intermediate journeys. It added much joy to the apostle's life that, while others were away and some had forsaken him, "the beloved physician" still remained with him. Others mentioned include Eubulus, Pudens, Linus, Claudia, and Onesiphorus.

"The Lord grant mercy to the house of Onesiphorus for he often refreshed me, and was not ashamed of my chains; but when he was in Rome, he eagerly searched for me, and found me—the Lord grant to him to find mercy form the Lord on that day—and you know very well what services he rendered at Ephesus" (2 Tim. 1:16–18, NASB).

His Longing for Timothy and Mark (2 Tim. 1:3–4; 4:9, 11, 21). Timothy was in Ephesus. Paul urged him to come to Rome before winter and to bring John Mark with him. He told Timothy to stop by Troas and pick up the cloak, the books, and the parchments which he left with Carpas.

PAUL'S FIRST TRIAL BEFORE THE ROMAN MAGISTRATES, AND HIS ACQUITTAL (2 TIM. 4:14–18)

The first defense (2 Tim. 4:16) is the first of the two hearings or trials which Paul had during his last imprisonment. We have no means of knowing the precise charge now made against the apostle.

It was dangerous even to appear in public as the friend or adviser of the apostle (2 Tim. 4:16). No advocate would venture to plead his cause, no procurator to aid him in arranging the evidence, no patron to appear as his supporter.

After the first trial nothing is certain. That he underwent execution by the sword is the tradition of antiquity, and would agree with the fact of his Roman citizenship, which would exempt him from death by torture. Of his last trial and death there is tradition only, but no history.

PAUL'S JOYOUS ANTICIPATION OF DEATH (2 TIM. 1:8–12; 2:8–13; 4:6–8)

Paul's last letter, 2 Timothy, brims with vitality and hope despite the bleak circumstances he faces. He is ready to depart this life and be with the Lord. And yet he cares about the progress of the gospel as much as if he were going to be around thirty more years. He points Timothy to the resources he will need to drawn on in running the race laid out for him. His metaphors are athletic and military—spurring Timothy on to his best.

PAUL'S DEATH

We have no details on the condemnation of Paul by the Roman court. It probably came quickly. Tradition outside the New Testament says Paul was beheaded.

SECTION FOUR: PAUL'S WRITINGS

Paul wrote thirteen letters in the New Testament. These were written over a period of less than twenty years. There are numerous theories about when and in what order these letters were written. For purposes of *Shepherd's Notes*, we are assuming a dating that has been widely accepted. This order is shown in the following chart. Paul's letters are then summarized in that chronological order.

"I remind you to kindle afresh the gift of God which is in you through the laying on of my hands. For God has not given us a spirit of timidity, but of power and love and discipline" (2 Tim. 1:6–7, NASB).

"So sin did its uttermost and its worst. Yet how poor and empty was its triumph! The blow of the axe only smote off the lock of the prison and let the spirit go forth to its home and to its crown. The city falsely called eternal dismissed him with execration from her gates; but then thousand times ten thousand welcomed him in the same hour at the gates of the city which is really eternal" —James A. Stalker from *The Life of St. Paul,* (Fleming H. Revell, 1950).

Paul's Writings and the Book of Acts

Book of Acts	Activity	Approximate Date	Writing
9:1–9	Paul's Conversion	A.D. 34–35	
9:26–29	Visit to Jerusalem	A.D. 37–38	
11:27–30	Second Visit to Jerusalem	A.D. 48	
13–14	First Mission (Cyprus and Galatia)	A.D. 48–50	Galatians
15	Jerusalem Council	A.D. 50	
16:1–18:22	Second Mission (Galatia, Macedonia, Greece)	A.D. 51–53	1, 2 Thessalonians
18:23–21:4	Third Mission (Ephesus, Macedonia, Greece)	A.D. 54–57	1, 2 Corinthians, Romans
21:15–26:32	Arrest in Jerusalem, trials and imprisonment in Caesarea	A.D. 58–60	
27–28	Voyage to Rome, Roman imprisonment	A.D. 61–63	Philemon, Colossians, Ephesians, Philippians
	Release, further work, final imprisonment, and death	A.D. 64	1 Timothy, Titus, 2 Timothy

GALATIANS

Background. There can be little doubt that the apostle Paul wrote the letter to the Galatians. This conclusion has seldom been called into question because the circumstances portrayed in the epistle, the details concerning Paul's life found in Galatians, and the theology of the book all coincide closely with information found in Acts and Paul's other letters. Galatians may have been written from Syrian Antioch in A.D. 48–49 or from Antioch, Corinth, Ephesus, or Macedonia in the early to mid–50s.

BASIC OUTLINE OF GALATIANS

I. Salutation and Preview of Themes (1:1–5)

II. Occasion: Condemnation of Error (1:6–9)

III. Defense of the Apostolic Authority of the Gospel Message (1:10–2:14)

IV. Statement of the Gospel Message Against the Backdrop of Jewish Legalism (2:15–21)

V. Explanation of the Meaning and Scriptural Basis of the Gospel Message (3:1–4:31)

OVERVIEW

Galatians is a passionate defense of the gospel not against those who directly denied it but who sought to add to it. Paul argues that the gospel is sufficient and that to add to it is to undermine it.

Summary of Contents. Paul faced two problems when he wrote Galatians. First, opponents attacked his authenticity as an apostle, and he wrote to defend his apostleship. Second, Paul's opponents preached a different gospel to the Galatians. A different gospel, which some of the Galatian Christians followed (1:6). So Paul wrote to discredit their gospel and to defend the truth of the gospel of Christ.

Paul gives such a fiery response to this disturbance. The Galatians are in danger of abandoning the gospel. In 1:1–5 Paul gives greetings to the churches, but he omits the statement of praise or thanksgiving that normally follows. Paul is too disturbed to give thanks or praise. Instead, in 1:6–9 Paul expresses distress at their fickle faith. The Galatians had received the one and true gospel but were turning away from it. In one of the strongest warnings in the Scripture, Paul pronounced a curse on those who preached something different from the gospel he had preached to them.

The major portion of the epistle (1:10–6:10) can be divided into three parts:

1. *Galatians 1:10–2:21.* In this section Paul defends his qualifications as an apostle against the attacks of the Judaizers. What Paul teaches and preaches is not his opinion. It isn't something he was taught by other humans. Christ Himself revealed this truth to Paul. When Paul met the apostles in Jerusalem they recognized and affirmed the truth of what Christ had revealed to Paul. This gospel is that both Jews and Gentiles are saved by the grace of God received by faith in Christ. The false teachers tried to convince the Galatians that in addition to faith in Christ, Gentiles had to become Jews

(and Gentile men must be circumcised) in order to be in right relationship with God.

2. *Galatians 3:1–5:12.* This section is the major argument of the epistle, where the differences between Paul's gospel and the Judaizer's heresy came to full light. Paul supports his thesis of faith alone on three principles: (1) the gift of the Spirit, (2) the promise and faith of Abraham, and (3) the curse of the law.

"But the fruit of the Spirit is love, joy, peace, kindness, goodness, faithfulness, gentleness and self-control. Against such things there is no law" (Gal. 5:22–23).

The gift of the Spirit came to them through faith, not the law. Abraham received the promise and righteousness by faith 430 years before the law was given. People of faith were true children of Abraham and heirs of the promise. Because people did not keep the law when it came, they fell under its curse. The law could only condemn sinners. Christ removed the curse of the law. The law was given as an interim provision until Christ came. Now He has come, and the believer is free. To turn back to the law was to return to slavery.

3. *Galatians 5:13–6:10.* In this final section, Paul argued that freedom from the law doesn't give a person license to sin. Christian freedom required the believer to walk by the Spirit, which was contrary to the desires and works of the flesh. Those who walk by the Spirit will yield the fruit of the Spirit. We find Paul's teaching on the fruit of the Spirit in Galatians 5:22–23. Paul closes (6:11–18), again urging them not to yield to circumcision and all it represented.

1 THESSALONIANS

---

1 THESSALONIANS IN A NUTSHELL

THEMES:	Salvation and Christ's return
PURPOSE:	To encourage new converts during persecution; to instruct them in Christian living and to assure them concerning the Second Coming
MAJOR DOCTRINES:	Last things
KEY PASSAGE:	4:13–16
OTHER KEY DOCTRINES:	Evangelism; prayer; God

BRIEF OUTLINE OF 1 THESSALONIANS
  I. Salutation (1:1)
 II. Personal Relations (1:2–3:13)
III. Church Problems (4:1–5:11)
IV. Concluding Exhortations (5:12–28)

OVERVIEW

Having received a report that they were growing in their faith, Paul writes this letter to answer the Thessalonians' questions, and to defend himself against enemies who are spreading false rumors. One key theme of the letter is the return of Christ.

Summary of Contents. The letter has two major sections: 1:1–3:13 and 4:1–5:28.

Background. Galatians probably was the first of Paul's letters to be written, and 1 Thessalonians was the second. Paul traveled to Thessalonica, the capital city of Macedonia, on his second missionary journey around A.D. 51. Luke reported the brief visit, Paul's preaching ministry there with Silas, and the subsequent persecution that drove them out of the city (Acts 17:1–9). Many people believed in Jesus Christ before they were compelled to leave. From Thessalonica, Paul went to Berea, Athens, and then Corinth. Timothy and Silas, who had been with Paul at Thessalonica, rejoined Paul in Corinth (Acts 18:5; 1 Thess. 3:6). Paul wrote 1 Thessalonians in response to Timothy's report shortly after his arrival.

1. *1 Thessalonians 1:1–3:13.* In this first major section, Paul is thankful for and reassuring toward the Thessalonians. He gives thanks for the Thessalonians' faithfulness (1:3–10). In fact, they had become models for believers in Macedonia and Achaia (1:7), turning from idols to "serve the living and true God" (1:9), and to await the coming of Christ from heaven (1:10).

2. *1 Thessalonians 4:1–5:28.* Among the problems the Thessalonian church faced were persecution by pagans (2:14) and a temptation for believers to accept pagan sexual standards (4:4–8). Some of the Christians seem to have given up working and to have relied on others to supply their needs (4:11–12). There was uncertainty about the fate of believers who had died, and some of the Thessalonians appear to have thought that Christ would come back soon and take them all to be with Him. What would happen to those who had died before the great event (4:13–18)? Paul's reply to this gives us information about Christ's return that we find nowhere else. Again, some of the believers seem to have been concerned about the time of Jesus' return (5:1–11). So Paul writes this pastoral letter to meet the needs of inexperienced Christians and to bring them closer to Christ.

The Nature of the Second Coming

We sorrow but with the assurance that death for a believer is only being "away from the body and at home with the Lord" (2 Cor. 5:8). In God's own time we will all be together eternally in the glorious family of God and "so we will be with the Lord forever" (1 Thess. 4:17).

2 THESSALONIANS

BRIEF OUTLINE OF 2 THESSALONIANS

I. Salvation (1:1–2)

II. Encouragement for the Church (1:3–12)

III. Instructions to Correct Misunderstandings (2:1–12)

IV. Injunctions to Steadfastness (2:13–3:18)

OVERVIEW

After learning that the believers at Thessalonica are unclear about what Paul had previously taught about future events, he writes this letter to provide them a fuller explanation.

Summary of Contents

1. *2 Thessalonians 1:1–12.* Following a brief introduction (1:1–2), Paul explains his prayer concerns

Background. Paul's authorship of 2 Thessalonians has had extremely strong support throughout church history. The interval between 1 and 2 Thessalonians must have been rather short, for the second epistle does not presuppose major changes in the inner constitution of the Thessalonian church or in the conditions under which Paul was writing.

for his readers. He expresses thanksgiving for their growth in faith and love for each other in spite of their intense sufferings (1:3–5). He assures his readers that he prays constantly that their way of living would ensure God's final commendation of their actions and life purpose (1:11–12).

2. *2 Thessalonians 2:1–17.* Paul then focuses on the topic of Christ's return. He uses the term "day of the Lord" to describe the complex of events that will occur at Jesus' return. He assures the Thessalonians that these events have not yet begun even though someone had used devious methods to suggest that the events were already unfolding (2:1–2). Paul insists that a large-scale rebellion against God and the appearance of the man of lawlessness will occur before the day of the Lord comes (2:3–4). This man of lawlessness will demand worship as God, work counterfeit miracles, and inspire all types of evil in his followers (2:5, 9–10). Those who follow him will face condemnation because they loved wickedness and accepted lies rather than divine truth (2:11–12). The display of power by the man of lawlessness will increase after the restrainer is removed (2:7). Jesus will render this lawless one utterly powerless at his return.

Not even the anticipation of Christ's return should lead Christians away from work. People able to work should earn their daily bread. Believers are to be exemplary in work, doing it as unto the Lord.

3. *2 Thessalonians 3:1–18.* Paul expresses some final concerns. One concern involves inappropriate conduct by some of the believers. Paul urges the Thessalonians to avoid a habit of idleness, settle into productive labor, and earn their own living (3:6–13).

Paul concludes his letter by reminding his readers that only divine strength would allow them to accomplish the goals he had set before them. He took the pen to add a personal greeting and provide a sign of authenticity for his letter.

1 CORINTHIANS

THEME:	Christian conduct in the church
PURPOSE:	To respond to questions about marriage, idol food, public worship; to discourage factions; to instruct on resurrection
MAJOR DOCTRINES:	The church; the resurrection
KEY PASSAGE:	12:31; 15:1–11
OTHER KEY DOCTRINES:	God; holiness; humanity

BASIC OUTLINE FOR 1 CORINTHIANS

I. Introduction (1:1–9)
II. Concerning Divisions (1:10–3:4)
III. Concerning Leadership (3:5–4:21)
IV. Concerning Immorality (5:1–6:20)
V. Concerning Marriage (7:1–40)
VI. Concerning Food Offered to Idols (8:1–11:1)
VII. Concerning Orderly Worship (11:2–34)
VIII. Concerning Spiritual Gifts (12:1–14:40)
IX. Concerning the Resurrection (15:1–58)
X. Concerning the Collection, and Closing Remarks (16:1–24)

Background. The letter (1:1–2; 16:21) as well as church tradition acknowledge Paul as the author of 1 Corinthians This affirmation generally has gone unchallenged. The letter was written around A.D. 55 near the end of Paul's three-year ministry in Ephesus (1 Cor. 16:5–9; Acts 20:31).

OVERVIEW

First Corinthians deals with a number of problems that have arisen in a church planted in a notoriously pagan culture.

Summary of Contents. Paul went to Corinth on his second missionary journey and began teaching immediately in the synagogue there. While some of the Jews believed, leaders and others of the synagogue rejected his witness. He continued his work through the home of Titius Justus, a Gentile who lived next door to the synagogue (Acts 18:7). Although Paul met resistance, the work went well and a struggling church began with even Crispus, the synagogue ruler and his family becoming Christians (Acts 18:7–8).

1. *1 Corinthians 1:1–9.* Paul expresses thanks for the spiritual gifts God has given to the Corinthians and for their exercise of those gifts.

2. *1 Corinthians 1:10–3:4.* Reports of divisions within the church have come to Paul from Chloe's family, and Paul addresses those divisions. The Corinthians were impressed by those who claimed to be wise. Paul contrasts the foolishness of God with the wisdom of man.

3. *1 Corinthians 3:5–4:21.* Human leaders play important roles in the church, but all of them are servants. Christ Jesus is the unchanging foundation of the church.

4. *1 Corinthians 5:1–6:20.* The sexual immorality on the part of one of the Corinthians is not something to boast about but a matter of profound grief and sorrow. The church should be

proactive in dealing with this brother with a view to bringing him to repentance.

5. *1 Corinthians 7:1–40.* God has ordained marriage and has set forth guidelines that make it a blessing. Paul's counsel is that not everyone should get married. Those who are married to an unbeliever should continue in that marriage.

6. *1 Corinthians 8:1–11:1.* Christians should think carefully about eating meat which has been offered to idols and then is sold in the market place. There is nothing intrinsically wrong with the meat, but many new Christians are offended when they see others participating in a practice that they see as contrary to their new life in Christ.

7. *1 Corinthians 11:2–34.* The Corinthians needed to give attention to their attitude and behavior in public worship, especially the Lord's Supper.

8. *1 Corinthians 12:1–14:40.* Spiritual gifts are imparted not to boost egos but for the good of the entire body of Christ. In this context, Paul says that the Corinthians should desire the greater gifts. Love should guide the exercising of spiritual gifts. In this context, Paul gives a beautifully detailed description of love.

9. *1 Corinthians 15:1–58.* Paul reminds the Corinthians of the basics of the gospel. Jesus' resurrection—well attested as a historical fact—is one of those basics without which there is no gospel. Jesus' resurrection is a picture and promise of the resurrection of all believers.

10. *1 Corinthians 16:1–24.* Paul will soon come for a visit. He and some of the Corinthians will then take the offering they have been collecting to the needy Christians in Jerusalem.

When considering an action, we have more than our own conscience to consider. We should consider the effect our action will have on the consciences of other believers.

2 CORINTHIANS

2 CORINTHIANS IN A NUTSHELL

THEME:	The nature of the gospel ministry
PURPOSE:	To prepare readers for Paul's third visit and to defend Paul and the gospel he taught against false teachers
MAJOR DOCTRINES:	The church; Jesus Christ; salvation
KEY PASSAGE:	5:11–6:2
OTHER KEY DOCTRINES:	God

Background. Paul is the author of this letter (1:1; 10:1). While it is a different kind of letter than Romans or even 1 Corinthians, it is characterized by his style. It contains more autobiographical material than any of his other writings. The letter is difficult to date, for we do not know the amount of time that separated 1 and 2 Coriathians. It has been variously dated between A.D. 55 and 57. The letter was penned at a difficult time between Paul and the Corinthians.

BRIEF OUTLINE OF 2 CORINTHIANS

   I. Introduction (1:1–2)
   II. Apostolic Experience (1:3–11)
   III. Apostolic Explanation (1:12–2:11)
   IV. Apostolic Ministry (2:12–7:16)
   V. Apostolic Fellowship (8:1–9:15)
   VI. Apostleship Defended (10:1–13:14)

OVERVIEW

2 Corinthians is the most personal and one of the most passionate of Paul's letters. Paul contrasts his own apostleship and his methods of doing Christ's work with those who sought to detract from his ministry among the Corinthians. The primary purpose of 2 Corinthians was to prepare the church at Corinth for another visit from Paul.

Summary of Contents. Second Corinthians has three major sections.

1. *2 Corinthians 1–7.* This first major section of the letter focuses on Paul's relationship with the Corinthians. That relationship has been strained for a number of reasons and Paul addresses these with a view toward reconciliation with the Corinthians. False apostles who claim to be superior to Paul have impressed the Corinthians. Paul takes this occasion to contrast his view of ministry and of the New Covenant itself with that of the false apostles.

Ministering in Christ's name involves suffering as well as victory. Paul's references to his own sufferings show that even the most faithful followers of Christ endure sufferings. Although He sustains the Christian who suffers, God does not always deliver the Christian from suffering.

2. *2 Corinthians 8–9.* In 1 Corinthians mentions the offering the Corinthians are collecting for the Christians in Jerusalem. In these chapters this theme re-emerges. Paul encouraged liberal, sacrificial giving on their part. He used other Gentile churches as examples to encourage generosity. Churches of Macedonia, for instance, had given sacrificially and joyfully (8:1–5). Of course, pivotal to the whole matter of giving for others was the self-giving of Christ (8:9). Paul fully expected the Corinthians to give sacrificially, pointing out to them that they would be blessed in the process (9:6–15).

3. *2 Corinthians 10–13.* Paul returns to the subject of his relationship with the Corinthians and responds to the criticism that has been directed against him.

ROMANS

BASIC OUTLINE FOR ROMANS

I. Introduction and Theme (1:1–17)
II. The Human Condition and God's Wrath (1:18–3:20)
III. Righteousness by Faith (3:21–4:25)
IV. God's Righteousness Explained (5:1–8:39)
V. God's Faithful Purposes for Jews and Gentiles (9:1–11:36)
VI. Righteousness for Christian Living and Service (12:1–15:13)
VII. Conclusion (15:14–16:27)

OVERVIEW

The theme of the letter is the gospel— "the power of God for salvation of everyone who believes" (1:16). Paul articulates the gospel and its practical implications for the church at Rome.

Background. Romans has been called the most important letter ever written. Paul wrote his letter to the Romans from Corinth during his third missionary journey around A.D. 56–57 (Acts 20:2–3).

Summary of Contents.

1. *Romans 1:1–17.* Paul's introduction to the letter (1:1–15) sets out the apostolic calling which qualifies him (vv. 1–7) and explains his reason for writing this letter (vv. 8–15). After the introduction, Paul crisply states the theme of his letter—the righteousness of God, revealed in the gospel and bringing salvation (1:16–17).

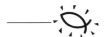

"Therefore no one will be declared righteous in his [God's] sight by observing the law; rather through the law we become conscious of sin" (Rom. 3:20).

2. *Romans 1:18–3:20.* Paul then supports his theme in the first major section of the letter by demonstrating that all persons need salvation, showing first that the power of sin rules the Gentiles (1:18–32) and, second, that the power of sin rules the Jews as well (2:1–3:8). Paul concludes this section with a summary statement that all humanity stands under the power of sin (3:19–20).

3. *Romans 3:21–4:25.* The second major section deals with God's provision of righteousness through Jesus Christ on the basis of faith. The question Paul deals with is how a holy, righteous God can be just and justify persons who have violated His law and have the ongoing tendency to do so. The answer is that God has taken the punishment for sin in His Son, Jesus. Those who have faith in Jesus' blood stand in right relationship with God.

4. *Romans 5:1–8:39.* After establishing the reality of justification by faith, Paul discusses, in the third section of Romans, the impact and implication of what God does for us in Christ and focuses on how salvation results in a victorious new life.

5. *Romans 9:1–11:36.* The salvation Christ brought raised profound questions among Jewish Christians about the destiny of the Jews who

still felt themselves to be God's people even though they had rejected Christ. Paul reminded his readers that Israel's rejection of the Messiah is not permanent. God's love of and election of Israel is irrevocable. Both Jews and Gentiles will receive mercy (11:1–36).

6. *Romans 12:1–15:13.* The final section is a summons to practical obedience to God.

7. *Conclusion* (Rom. 15:14–16:27). In the conclusion to the letter, Paul summarized his ministry and his plans for the future, requesting their prayers (15:14–33). Then he commended Phoebe (16:1–2), sent greetings to individual Christians (16:3–24), and ended his letter with praise for God (16:27).

PHILEMON

PHILEMON IN A NUTSHELL

THEME:	Christian fellowship
PURPOSE:	To effect reconciliation between a runaway slave and his Christian master
MAJOR DOCTRINES:	Christian ethics
KEY PASSAGE:	8–16
OTHER KEY DOCTRINES:	Prayer; the church; discipleship

BASIC OUTLINE OF PHILEMON

I. The Salutation (vv. 1–3)
II. Prayer of Thanksgiving for Philemon (vv. 4–7)
III. A Good Word on Behalf of Onesimus (vv. 8–21)
IV. Paul's Personal Request (v. 22)
V. Greetings and Benediction (vv. 23–25)

OVERVIEW

Paul writes to Philemon telling him that his runaway slave, Onesimus, has come to faith in Christ. Paul urges Philemon to forgive Onesimus and accept him back as a brother in Christ.

Summary of Contents. Paul's only epistle of a private and personal nature that is included in the New Testament was written to Philemon in A.D.

Background. Philemon is closely linked with the epistle to the Colossians. The letter was carried by Onesimus to Philemon with Tychicus (Col. 4:7–9; Eph. 6:21–22). The letter was written near the end of Paul's first Roman imprisonment at the same time as Ephesians and Colossians, about A.D. 60–61.

61. Philemon's slave, Onesimus, had robbed him and escaped to Rome. There under the preaching of Paul, Onesimus came to faith in Christ. Paul wrote to Philemon concerning Onesimus and sent the letter along with Onesimus back to Philemon in Colosse. Paul asked Philemon to forgive and receive Onesimus not as a slave but as a brother (v.16). This request was not made from Paul's apostolic authority but tenderly as a Christian friend. Paul wrote, "Receive him as myself" (v.17, KJV).

Paul also stated that he was willing to pay any damages caused by Onesimus.

EPHESIANS

BASIC OUTLINE FOR EPHESIANS

I. Introduction (1:1–2)
II. God's Purposes in Christ (1:3–3:21)
III. God's Purposes in the Church (4:1–6:20)
IV. Conclusion (6:21–24)

OVERVIEW

Christ in His church and the church in Christ is the theme of Ephesians. Ephesians is also a manual of Christian living. It pulls together much of the material of the other letters of the New Testament, but in a more concise form. Ephesians gives some practical advice for spiritual growth and development.

Summary of Contents. The letter has a salutation (1:1–2), two major sections (1:3–3:21 and 4:1–6:20), and a conclusion (6:21–24). A

Background. The early church viewed Paul (1:1; 3:1) as author of Ephesians even though this letter contains a writing style, vocabulary, and even some teachings that are not typical of the apostle. Paul penned the letter while in prison (3:1; 4:1; 6:20). Paul most likely wrote Colossians, Philemon, and Philippians during the same imprisonment. It is plausible to suggest that Paul wrote the letter from Rome around A.D. 60–61.

doxology (3:20–21) denotes the division between the two major sections, although both sections have some common themes.

1. *Ephesians 1:13–3:21.* Paul begins by praising God for His grace in Christ. This grace was not an afterthought that God came up with in response to Adam's sin. This has been God's plan from the beginning. God—Father, Son, and Spirit—not only conceived the plan prior to creation, but is ever at work to effect this plan. They key moment in this plan is Jesus' shedding His blood to provide forgiveness of sins and redemption from sin.

Jesus' death took place outside us. But His death takes effect in our lives as we hear and believe the gospel. At the same time, God's Spirit sets His seal on us, indicating God now owns us and promises to fully carry out His purposes in us for time and eternity.

2. *Ephesians 4:1–6:2.* Paul now looks at the practical implications of being in Christ. Ethical imperatives dominate the section. While believers are different and have diverse gifts, there is a unity that binds them together—one body, one Spirit, one hope, one Lord, one faith, one baptism, one God and Father.

To complete his letter, Paul calls his readers to put on God's armor to avoid Satan's schemes. This leads to a life that seeks God's blessing for oneself and for other servants of God and which is active in encouraging ones fellow believers.

The apostle teaches that Jewish and Gentile believers are one in Christ. This oneness is to be demonstrated by their love for one another. Paul uses the noun form of the verb "to love" (*agape*) nineteen times (about one-sixth of the total uses in all of Paul's letters). *Agape* love is an unconditional love that puts the other's interests ahead of one's own. Ephesians begins with love (1:4–6) and ends with love (6:23–24).

COLOSSIANS

COLOSSIANS IN A NUTSHELL

THEME:	The supremacy of Christ in all things
PURPOSE:	To oppose false teachings related to a matter and spirit dualism and to stress the complete adequacy of Christ
MAJOR DOCTRINES:	Jesus Christ
KEY PASSAGE:	1:15–23
OTHER KEY DOCTRINES:	The church; prayer; God

BASIC OUTLINE OF COLOSSIANS
   I. Introduction (1:1–14)
   II. Explanation of the Supremacy of Christ (1:15–23)
   III. Ministry for the Church (1:24–2:5)
   IV. Warnings Against False Spirituality (2:6–3:4)
   V. Exhortations for Ethical Living (3:5–4:6)
   VI. Conclusion (4:17–18)

Background. Tradition supports the letter's claim that Paul was the author (Col. 1:1). Paul had never been to Colosse, but he wrote to them to address matters raised by Epaphras (1:7). The letter would have been written about the same time as Ephesians and Philemon (around A.D. 60–61).

OVERVIEW

This short letter proclaims the supremacy and sufficiency of Christ. Paul was writing for a context where Christ was proclaimed but He was seen as only part of God's revelation and plan for redemption. Paul asserted that when a person has Christ, he has the very fullness of God.

Summary of Contents

1. *Colossians 1:3–2:23.* This doctrinal section begins with a description of the grandeur of the preeminent Christ (1:15–20). Though the precise meaning of some words and phrases is uncertain, there is no doubt as to Paul's intent. He means to present Jesus as fully God incarnate (1:15, 19), as supreme Lord over all creation (vv. 15, 17), as supreme Lord of the church (v. 18), and as the only Source of reconciliation (v. 20).

Becoming and being a Christian.

Being Christian continues on the same basis as we began, faith in Christ. He reveals Himself to us, changes us, delivers us, and leads us only in response to our continued trust. Our response is to answer His love and faithfulness with our own.

2. *Colossians 3:1–4:17.* Chapters 3–4 exhort believers to live out the new life made possible by Christ's work of redemption set forth in the first two chapters.

Rules for the household appear in 3:18–4:1. The typical first-century household is assumed, thus the passage addresses wives and husbands, fathers and children, masters and slaves.

A final group of exhortations (4:2–6) and an exchange of greetings (4:7–17) bring the letter to a close.

PHILIPPIANS IN A NUTSHELL

THEME:	Joy in Christ
PURPOSE:	To commend Ephaphroditus; to affirm generosity; to encourage unity, humility, and faithfulness even to death
MAJOR DOCTRINES:	Christian unity; joy in salvation
KEY PASSAGE:	1:3–11
OTHER KEY DOCTRINES:	Christian ethics; prayer; God

BASIC OUTLINE OF PHILIPPIANS

I. Greetings (1:1–2)

II. Paul's joyful concern for the church (1:3–11)

III. Paul's joyful response in the midst of difficult circumstances (1:12–26)

IV. Paul's personal plea for Christian unity and humility (1:27–2:18)

V. Paul's pastoral commendation for his co-workers and their examples of humility (2:19–30)

VI. Paul's warning against the error of self-righteousness (3:1–11)

VII. Paul's single-minded exhortation to Christian maturity (3:12–4:1)

VIII. Paul's gentle advice for joy and peace among the saints (4:2–9)

Background.
Philippians was written while the apostle Paul was in prison, probably from Rome about A.D. 62.

IX. Paul's genuine thanksgiving for the church's generosity (4:10–20)

X. Conclusion (4:21–23)

OVERVIEW

Philippians is the most personal letter Paul wrote to a church.

Summary of Contents. As a highly personal letter, Philippians lacks the structure that some of Paul's letters have.

1. *Philippians 1:1–30.* The very thought of these believers in Philippi causes Paul to thank God for them. They are precious to him and he longs to see them. Because he loves them so, he prays for their continued growth in Christ (1:3–11). He wants them to know about his situation as a prisoner of Rome (1:12–26). His captors are being evangelized (vv. 12–13). His compatriots have gained confidence through his bold example (v.14). Even the brethren who are working with wrong motives are sharing the good news actively. Paul rejoices in their work (15–18). Paul seems, on balance, to be hopeful about being released and being reunited with the Philippians, but he does convey to them that he has looked death straight in the eye and isn't afraid of it. After all, death will bring him into the full presence of Christ. The downside of death is that, for a time, Paul will be separated from the Philippians and can't do for them what he would like.

The joy of the Lord is not dependent on circumstances or people. It comes from a deep and abiding relationship with Jesus Christ. Life's goal, and also death's, is to exalt Christ (1:19–25). Cultural roots and past history are not so important as the desire to know Christ in fuller and deeper ways (3:1–11). "I can do everything through him who gives me strength" (4:13).

2. *Philippians 2:1–30.* When Paul returned to Philippi, he hoped to find a church united in Christ. Philippians 1:27–4:9 is a multifaceted call for unity in the church. The great cause of

the proclamation of the gospel calls for them to be united in spirit, in task, and in confidence (1:27–30). Their common Christian experience (2:1) and purpose (2:2) should also rule out a self-centered, self-serving attitude (2:3–4). Those who follow Christ must follow him in selfless service to others (2:5–11).

3. *Philippians 3:1–21.* The tone of the letter changes in chapter 3. The encouragement to rejoice (3:1) unexpectedly becomes a stern warning (3:2). A problem was threatening the church at Philippi which had the potential of destroying the foundation of unity and the basis of joy. The exact nature of the problem is unclear. Jewish legalism (3:2–11), Christian or *gnostic* perfectionism (3:12–16), and pagan libertinism (3:17–21) are all attacked.

4. *Philippians 4:1–23.* Chapter 4 returns to a more positive instruction and affirmation of the church. Two women, Euodias and Syntyche (4:2–3), were exhorted to end their conflict, for personal disagreements may be as damaging to the unity of the church as false doctrine.

Philippians 2:6–11 is known as the *kenosis* passage (from the Greek word translated "emptied" in 2:7, RSV). The language and structure of the passage have convinced most commentators that Paul was quoting a hymn which was already in use in the church. The purpose of the pre-Pauline hymn was probably to teach the believer about the nature and work of Christ. Preexistence, incarnation, passion, resurrection, and exaltation are all summarized in a masterful fashion. In the context of Philippians, however, the *kenosis* passage is used to highlight the humility and selfless service demonstrated by Jesus, whose example the Christian is to follow.

1 Timothy

THEMES:	Church organization; the importance of sound doctrine; and the refutation of false doctrine
PURPOSE:	To encourage Timothy as a minister, to refute false doctrine, and to instruct about church organization and leadership
MAJOR DOCTRINES:	Church leaders
KEY PASSAGE:	3:1–15
OTHER KEY DOCTRINES:	God; Christian ethics; salvation

BASIC OUTLINE OF FIRST TIMOTHY:

I. Introduction (1:1–2)

II. Warning Against False Teachers (1:3–30)

III. Guidelines for Church Worship (2:1–15)

VI. Instructions for Church Leadership (3:1–13)

V. Maintaining the Truth (3:14–4:16)

VI. Miscellaneous Instructions for the Church (5:1–6:10)

VII. Personal Charge to Timothy (6:11–21)

OVERVIEW

Paul encourages Timothy in his ministry in Ephesus, urging him to remain faithful, giving him instruction about dealing with false doctrine, matters of church organization, and administration.

Background. Paul's three letters to Timothy and Titus are called the Pastoral Letters. These letters were written near the end of Paul's life between A.D. 64 and 67 to guide his two younger associates.

Summary of Contents. The following breaks down Paul's first letter to Timothy according to its chapters:

1. *1 Timothy 1.* Paul writes as an apostle of Jesus Christ with the authority of Christ.

He urges Timothy to deal forthrightly with false teaching in the church at Ephesus. The error described in verses 3–4 was Jewish in nature. Some were falsely teaching a mythological treatment of Old Testament genealogies. This teaching was generating a lot of meaningless controversy. Timothy was urged to teach "sound doctrine" in its place (1:10–11).

2. *1 Timothy 2.* Paul shows the priority of prayer in the worship services of the church. Seven different Greek words appear in the New Testament for prayer, and four of them occur in verse 1. One of the most significant statements in the entire New Testament is found in verse 5. Paul wrote there is "one God" and "one mediator between God and men, the man Christ Jesus." Monotheism is clearly taught as opposed to the polytheism of the first-century religious world. *Mediator* is a word that means "go-between." Jesus is humanity's "go-between" to God. He is also called our "ransom" in verse 6. A ransom was paid to a slave owner to purchase the freedom

Today's church is to seek as leaders persons ready to walk the high road spiritually and morally.

of the slave. Jesus paid for our redemption with His death on the cross.

3. *1 Timothy 3*. Fifteen moral and ethical requirements are mentioned in verses 2–7.

4. *1 Timothy 4*. Paul affirms that "everything God created is good" (4:4). Some false teachers maintained that marriage and certain foods were wrong. Paul drew from the message of Genesis in which God affirmed everything He created was good! It is man who takes God's good creation and corrupts it. The apostle reminded Timothy to be a "good minister of Christ Jesus" (4:6) and to "set an example for the believers in speech, in life, in love, in faith and in purity" (4:12).

5. *1 Timothy 5*. Paul gives practical instructions concerning the ministry of the church to various groups that comprise its membership.

6. *1 Timothy 6*. The teachers of false doctrine were motivated by "financial gain" (6:5). Paul warns in light of this fact and others that "the love of money is a root of all kinds of evil" (6:10).

TITUS

BASIC OUTLINE OF TITUS:

I. Introduction (1:1–4)
II. The Appointment of Elders (1:5–9)
III. The Rebuke of False Teachers (1:10–16)
IV. The Different Groups in the Church (2:1–15)
V. The Responsibility of Christian Living (3:1–11)
VI. Personal Concluding Requests (3:12–15)

OVERVIEW

Paul has left Titus in Crete to complete the work begun there. This is a follow-up letter to Titus giving him encouragement and specific instructions.

Summary of Contents.

1. Titus 1. Titus's first duty was to appoint elders. The qualifications listed in verses 6–9 are similar to those mentioned in 1 Timothy 3:1–7. False

Background. There is good evidence that Paul was released from his first imprisonment at Rome. Between this and his last imprisonment, Paul and Titus worked on Crete leading many to faith in Christ. This letter to Titus was written in the mid 60s.

teachers threatened the church. He mentions the "circumcision group" (1:10), a reference to converts to the Christian faith from Judaism who apparently taught that the rite of circumcision was necessary to be a complete Christian. This group of teachers and all who sought to lead the people astray were corrupt in their minds and detestable in their actions (1:15–16).

2. *Titus* 2. Paul urges Titus to teach "sound doctrine" to correct the false teaching. Proper teaching will lead to proper conduct in the lives of believers.

3. *Titus* 3. Paul reminds the believers "to be subject to rulers and authorities" (3:1). The subjection is to be voluntary because the institution of government was created by God. The believers were to treat all persons with consideration and humility. The letter concludes with some practical instructions for Titus. Zenas, the lawyer, and Apollos probably delivered the letter to Titus (3:13).

2 TIMOTHY

---

2 TIMOTHY IN A NUTSHELL

THEME:	Church organization and refutation of false doctrine
PURPOSE:	To encourage Christians in the face of persecution and false doctrine
MAJOR DOCTRINES:	Education
KEY PASSAGE:	2:14–19
OTHER KEY DOCTRINES:	Evil and suffering; Jesus Christ; prayer

---

BASIC OUTLINE OF SECOND TIMOTHY:
   I. Introduction (1:1–7)
  II. Suffering and the Gospel (1:8–18)
 III. Encouragement to Faithfulness (2:1–13)
 IV. Contrasts in the Church (2:14–26)
  V. Godlessness in the Last Days (3:1–9)
 VI. Final Advice to Timothy (3:10–4:18)
VII. Final Greetings (4:19–22)

Background. This may well have been Paul's last letter. The letter contains Paul's stirring words of encouragement and instruction to his young disciple. Paul longed to see Timothy (1:4) and asked him to come to Rome for a visit. It is generally believed that Timothy went.

OVERVIEW

Paul urges Timothy to be faithful, to endure the difficulties, and to fulfill his calling as a preacher of the gospel. He foresees the end of his own missionary career in martyrdom (4:6–8). The situation was made more difficult by Demas's desertion of the missionary enterprise (4:10) and by Alexander the coppersmith, who hurt Paul deeply (4:14).

Summary of Contents. The following breaks down Paul's second letter to Timothy according to its chapters:

1. *2 Timothy 1.* Paul reminded Timothy of his heritage in the faith—a faith that first lived in his grandmother Lois and in his mother Eunice (1:5). Paul had become Timothy's father in the ministry (1:2). Timothy may have been a naturally timid person. Because of this, Paul told him to minister with "a spirit of power" (1:7). The Holy Spirit empowers believers, but we should be careful to exercise this power in a "spirit ... of love and of self-discipline" (1:7). Two men, Phygelus and Hermogenes, deserted Paul (1:15). Onesiphorus was a refreshing friend and not ashamed of Paul's chains (1:16).

2. *2 Timothy 2.* Paul urges Timothy to be strong in Jesus Christ. Paul used the metaphors of a good soldier, athlete, and a hard-working farmer when describing the Christian's calling. The purpose of that calling is so all "may obtain the salvation that is in Christ Jesus" (2:10). Timothy was to be one who "correctly handles the word of truth" (2:15) in the face of those who mishandled it. Hymenaeus (1 Tim. 1:20) and

Philetus were singled out. They were teaching that the resurrection had already taken place and were destroying the faith of some (2:18).

3. *2 Timothy 3*. Paul's reference to "the last days" is a reference to the second coming of Jesus. The days preceding His return will be "terrible." Characteristics of these last days have appeared in many different ages, but the times before Jesus' actual return will be even more intense.

4. *2 Timothy 4*. Paul further instructs Timothy to be prepared to "preach the Word" at all times. The need is paramount, for people will not always adhere to "sound doctrine" (4:3). Paul, drawing on the imagery of Numbers 28:24, compared his life to that of a "drink offering." This was poured on a sacrifice before it was offered. He was ready to depart this life and go to be with the Lord. He anticipated the "crown of righteousness" that awaited him (4:8). The letter closes with practical instructions and pastoral remarks for Timothy.

The following list is a collection of the source works used for this volume on the life and writings of Paul. All, except the work by Frank Goodwin, are from Broadman & Holman's list of published reference resources. These are provided to accommodate the reader's need for more specific information and for an expanded treatment of the scriptural accounts. All of these works will greatly aid in the reader's study, teaching, and presentation of the truths of Paul's letters. The accompanying annotations can be helpful in guiding the reader to the proper resources.

RESOURCES:

Adams, J. McKee, and Rev. Joseph A. Callaway, *Biblical Backgrounds*. This work provides valuable information on the physical and geographical settings of the New Testament. Its many color maps and other features add depth and understanding to the Gospel narratives.

Blair, Joe, *Introducing the New Testament*. A high-level overview of the New Testament books that contain outlines of books, special graphics, maps, photos, and summary questions.

Goodwin, Frank J., *A Harmony of the Life of St. Paul* (According to the Acts of the Apostles and the Pauline Epistles) (New York: American Tract Society). A classic study of the life of Paul. The author provides a correspondence of the book of Acts with the Pauline epistles, and attempts to harmonize the accounts. The result is a unique perspective on Paul's life and ministry as well as the growth and expansion of the early church.

Holman Bible Dictionary. An exhaustive, alphabetically arranged resource of Bible-related subjects. An excellent tool of definitions and other information on the people, places, things, and events.

Holman Bible Handbook. A comprehensive treatment of the Gospels that offers outlines, commentary on key themes and sections, and full-color photos, illustrations, charts, and maps. Provides an accent on the broader theological teachings. Various selections were used throughout the book of Acts.

Holman Book of Biblical Charts, Maps, and Reconstructions. A colorful, visual collection of charts, maps, and reconstructions, These well-designed tools are invaluable to the study of the Bible.

Lea, Thomas D., *The New Testament: Its Background and Message.* An excellent resource for background material—political, cultural, historical, and religious. Provides background information in both broad strokes on specific books, including the Gospels.

Shepherds' Notes for *Romans, Galatians, Ephesians, Philippians, Colossians, Philemon, 1 & 2 Corinthians, 1 & 2 Thessalonians, 1 & 2 Timothy, Titus.* Shepherd's Notes are study volumes that deliver the essentials of each book of the Bible in succinct, easy-to-digest bites.